HOW THE WORLD WORKS
RELIGION

*The rich history of the
world's major faiths*

John Hawkins

SIRIUS

This edition published in 2019 by Sirius Publishing, a division
of Arcturus Publishing Limited, 26/27 Bickels Yard,
151–153 Bermondsey Street, London SE1 3HA

Original authors:
Judaism & Islam by Cath Senker
Christianity & Sikhism by Jane Bingham
Hinduism by Rasamandala Das
Buddhism by Anita Ganeri

Edited by JMS Books llp
Layout by Chris Bell

ISBN: 978-1-78888-351-1
AD004859UK

Printed in Malaysia

CONTENTS

INTRODUCTION
THE ROOTS OF FAITH

No one can say for sure how religion began. According to one theory, it developed as a kind of glue to hold societies together. To keep everyone cooperating, it would have helped to develop a belief system that promoted unselfish behaviour. It's also possible that religion came about as an attempt to develop some sort of relationship with the natural forces that governed people's lives – a kind of contract or agreement – so that the sun would keep rising and the supply of fish or game would not diminish. Perhaps it arose partly out of a sense of wonder at the beauty and complexity of the natural world, and the incredible fact of existence. For early humans, along with self-awareness must have come a desire to make sense of the world, to tell stories that could help to explain it.

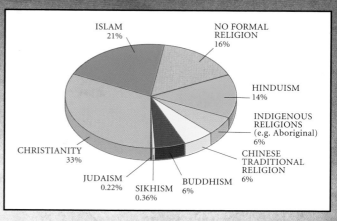

Right: *Pie chart showing the distribution of world faiths.*

Exactly when religion began is, again, impossible to say, but evidence of religious practice begins to crop up in the archaeological record during the Upper Palaeolithic (50,000–10,000 years ago). The discovery in a German cave of a 40,000-year-old figurine of a lion-headed man carved from the tusk of a woolly mammoth, suggests the development of some form of mythology by this stage. And evidence of an early belief in an afterlife was found at a burial site in Sungir, Russia, dating from between 28,000 and 30,000 years ago. As well as human remains, the grave contained jewellery, clothing and spears, begging the question: why bury someone with these valued items unless it was to aid them in their life after death? Finds like these have been made all over the world. Clearly, religious belief is a universal trait common to all human cultures.

Scholars use the term animism to describe the simple forms of faith that may have been practised by our early ancestors. Animists believe that non-human entities, whether animals, plants or celestial objects, possess a spiritual essence. Gradually, over the past 5,000 years, these animist ideas began to evolve into the more complex systems of belief we know

as religion. From the notion that the sun is a god emerged the idea that the sun is controlled by a god (anthropomorphic animism). Each religion acquired its own narratives, symbols, morality and forms of worship. Priesthoods, scriptures and temples were developed, and holy sites and sacred relics came into being. The first religions were almost always polytheistic. Zoroastrianism, with its worship of a single Supreme Being, Ahura Mazda, was an exception.

The great religions of today emerged in the Middle East and India, offering messages powerful enough to attract millions of believers. This book traces the history of these religions from their origins to the present day. It looks at the people who founded and guided them, the events that shaped them, the rich heritage of philosophy, culture, art and scripture that they inspired, and the rituals, customs and festivals that have made these faiths a living experience for millions of people.

CHAPTER 1
JUDAISM

JUDAISM is not just a religion. The Jewish people are an ethnic group: everyone who has a Jewish mother is considered Jewish, whether they practise the religion or not. Consequently, the history of the Jewish religion is also the history of the Jewish people. Jews believe they are descended from a tribe of people that lived in the ancient land of Canaan, which encompasses most of modern Israel, Palestine, Jordan and Syria. The story of the origins of the Jews, who were also known as Israelites or Hebrews in ancient times, is found in the Torah, a sacred text containing the first five books of the Bible. According to the first book, Genesis, the original ancestor of the Jewish people was a man called Abraham.

Abraham and the Israelites

In around 1800 BCE, Abraham and his clan left Ur in Mesopotamia (modern-day Iraq) and travelled to Canaan. Abraham had a son, Isaac, who in turn fathered Jacob. Jacob's twelve sons founded the twelve tribes of Israel. Owing to a severe famine in Canaan, some of the tribes settled in Egypt, where they were enslaved. Several generations later, according to the Book of Exodus, a great leader called Moses led the Israelites out of slavery and to freedom in Canaan.

There is some archaeological evidence for the biblical account of Abraham's migration. Between 2000 and 1500 BCE, a nomadic group called the Amorites invaded Mesopotamia, which led to the decline of Ur. This may have prompted Abraham's departure from the region.

Scholars disagree about the flight from Egypt to Canaan, however. While some believe that the Israelites left Egypt in one mass migration, as stated in the Bible, others argue that a more gradual settlement of Canaan was more likely.

The mitzvoth and the Halacha

The Israelites gradually formed one nation with a set of strong religious principles. They were united by their belief in an all-powerful God who created the universe. They believed that Moses received the Torah directly from God and that the Israelites had a covenant with God: God would look after them if they followed the *mitzvoth* (commandments) in the Torah.

The *mitzvoth* lay down the rules of behaviour for all areas of Jewish religious and daily life. For example, Jews must eat

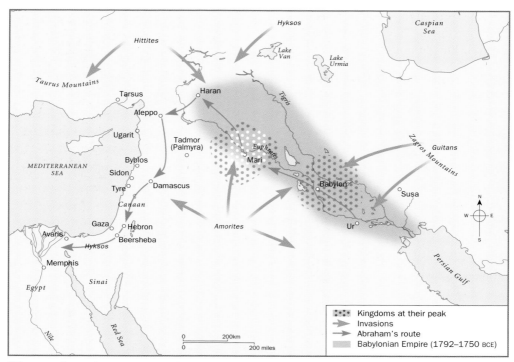

This map shows the emergence of the Jewish people between around 2000 and 1000 BCE. According to the Bible, Abraham, Isaac and Jacob lived in Beersheba, in modern-day southern Israel.

kosher food – food that has been prepared so that it is suitable under Jewish law. Jews must also keep *Shabbat*, or the Sabbath, as a day of prayer and rest. God also gave Moses the *Halacha*, the oral Torah, which explained how the commandments were to be kept. The *Halacha* was handed down the generations by word of mouth.

The kingdom of Israel

The Torah describes how the twelve Israelite tribes in Canaan were ruled by councils of elders in peacetime. During wartime, each tribe was led by a judge, who was a tribal chieftain. Many wars were fought. The most powerful enemies of the Israelites were the Philistines, who had established themselves in the southern coastal plain of Canaan by the end of the 11th century BCE. They frequently attacked the Israelite tribes. As separate tribes, the Israelites proved too weak to repel the Philistine threat. They eventually united into one kingdom, the kingdom of Israel.

According to the Book of Exodus, Moses parted the waves of the sea so that the Israelites could escape from Egypt.

HEBRON, HOLY CITY

According to Genesis, Abraham's wife Sarah died in Hebron. Abraham purchased a cave and the surrounding field as a burial place for her. The tomb is also believed to be the burial place of Abraham, Isaac, Jacob and their wives (except for Jacob's wife Rachel, who was buried near Bethlehem). The site, near the modern city of Hebron in the West Bank, is holy to Jews, Christians and Muslims, who all see Abraham as their ancestor.

So Ephron's field in Machpelah near Mamre – both the field and the cave in it, and all the trees within the borders of the field – was legally made over to Abraham as his property in the presence of all the Hittites [a local clan] who had come to the gate of the city. Afterwards Abraham buried his wife Sarah in the cave in the field of Machpelah near Mamre (which is at Hebron) in the land of Canaan.

Genesis 23:17–19

The Israelites under the kings

The kingdom of Israel lasted from around 1000 BCE to 586 BCE. The first king was Saul, who defeated many enemies and checked the advance of the Philistines. Saul was succeeded by David, who crushed the Philistines and conquered the city of Jerusalem, which he made his capital. Jerusalem became the spiritual focus of the Jewish religion. David's successor, Solomon, created a powerful kingdom and brought peace and prosperity. He built fortified towns and the magnificent First Temple in Jerusalem.

Despite having a reputation for wisdom, Solomon sowed the seeds of division in the kingdom, for example, by taxing all the tribes except his own tribe of Judah. After his death in 928 BCE, the northern tribes rebelled and set up their own kingdom, named Israel, while the southern tribes stayed loyal to Solomon's son and established the kingdom of Judah.

Destruction of the kingdoms

In 722 BCE, the Assyrians (from Mesopotamia) captured Samaria, the capital of Israel. Israel was absorbed into the Assyrian Empire and its population was deported to Mesopotamia. The exiled people became known as the ten lost tribes of Israel. During the following century,

This description of Solomon's kingdom at its height is from the Bible:

Judah and Israel were many, as the sand which is by the sea, in multitude, eating and drinking, and making merry. And Solomon reigned over all kingdoms from the river [Euphrates] unto the land of the Philistines, and unto the border of Egypt: they brought presents, and served Solomon all the days of his life.... For he had dominion over all the region on this side of the river ... and he had peace on all sides around him.... And Solomon's wisdom excelled all the wisdom of all the children of the east country, and all the wisdom of Egypt ... and his fame was in all nations round about.

1 Kings 4:20–31

This detail from a fresco by Michelangelo in the Sistine Chapel in Rome depicts the Prophet Ezekiel. Ezekiel was one of the Israelites exiled to Babylonia after the Babylonians conquered Judah in 586 BCE. He prophesised that the Israelites would return to their homeland.

The shaded area of this map shows the kingdom of Israel under King Solomon in around 970–928 BCE. King Solomon built the fortified towns, including Megiddo, Hazor, Gezer and Beth-Horon, to withstand sieges and protect his kingdom. Under his rule, trade with neighbouring lands increased.

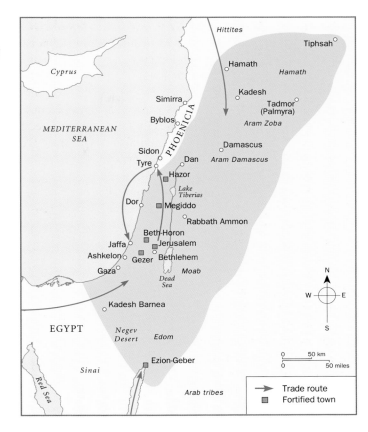

the Assyrian Empire declined, and Babylon, a city in Mesopotamia, grew stronger. In 586 BCE, the Babylonians conquered Jerusalem, destroyed Solomon's Temple and ended the kingdom of Judah. The Israelites were captured or sent into exile in Babylon, where they formed an organized community and preserved their Jewish identity.

Under the Persian Empire

In 538 BCE, King Cyrus the Great of Persia (modern-day Iran) conquered Babylonia (southern Mesopotamia). He allowed all the people exiled by the Babylonians to return to their homelands, including the Jews. Most Jews chose to stay in Babylon, where they are thought to have enjoyed a fairly prosperous life. Around 50,000 Jews returned, in several waves, to Jerusalem. They rebuilt the city and, in 516 BCE, began reconstructing the Temple.

There was friction between the returning Israelites and those who had remained. The returning exiles found that the Jews in Jerusalem had become lax – they were not following the Torah laws and many had married non-Jews. Around the fifth century BCE, the religious leaders Ezra and Nehemiah reinstated Jewish law in Judah. The Jews renewed their covenant with God, vowing not to work on the Sabbath, to pay a tax to support the Temple and not to marry non-Jews.

Hellenism

The next major upheaval in the fortunes of the Israelites occurred when Alexander the Great defeated the Persians in 333 BCE, then conquered Judah the following year. Alexander was from Macedonia in northern Greece, and he and his successors promoted Greek culture within their empire. Many Jews became attracted to Hellenic ways. They started to speak Greek and abandoned their traditions. Hostility developed between Hellenist and traditional Jews.

A hanukiah (nine-branched candlestick) at the Western Wall in Jerusalem, lit for the festival of Hanukkah, which celebrates the restoration of the Jewish Temple in 164 BCE.

The Maccabees

The tensions between Greek and Jewish traditions led to a revolt in the second century BCE. At this time, the Seleucid kings (descended from Alexander the Great's general Seleucus) dominated Judah, and tried to Hellenize Jerusalem. Between 175 and 163 BCE, Seleucid king Antiochus IV robbed the Temple, banned the Jewish practice of circumcision and forbade Jews from observing the Sabbath and reading the Torah. Antiochus announced that the Temple would be rededicated to the Greek god Zeus, and that animals – including pigs, which were considered unclean by Jews – would be sacrificed there. Led by Judah the Maccabee, the Jews rebelled. In 164 BCE, they recaptured Jerusalem and restored the Temple, an event celebrated at the festival of *Hanukkah*. Judah's family, the Hasmoneans, founded a dynasty that ruled for the following one hundred years.

The Romans

In 63 BCE, the Romans conquered the land of Israel. At first they allowed the Hasmoneans to continue to rule in Judah. However, in 37 BCE, Herod, whom the Romans had appointed king of Judea (the Roman name for Judah) three years earlier, laid siege to Jerusalem and destroyed the Hasmonean dynasty. He executed many Jewish leaders who had been loyal to the Hasmoneans. Although Herod rebuilt the Temple in Jerusalem, he was still hated as a cruel foreign ruler.

In 6 CE, Judea came under direct Roman rule. Between 66 and 73 CE, Jewish rebel groups fought the Roman authorities. In 70 CE, the Romans regained control over Jerusalem, and burned down the Second Temple (which had replaced the first). All that remained was the Western Wall.

A final Jewish revolt led by Simon Bar Kochba in 132 CE drove the Romans out of Jerusalem. But in 135 CE, they reconquered the city and enslaved its population. By this time, most of the Jews had left Judea, which the Romans had renamed Palestine. They had dispersed to different lands in what became known as the diaspora, a Greek word meaning 'scattering'.

Judaism after the Temple

The destruction of the Temple was a disaster for the Jewish people. They lost the central focus of their religious practice. Yet wherever Jewish people went, they maintained their traditions. After the fall of Jerusalem in 70 CE, a group of scholars living in Yavneh, in modern-day central Israel, re-established the *Sanhedrin*. Formerly in Jerusalem, this was the supreme Jewish legal and religious council for Palestine and the diaspora. The scholars began to develop a Jewish legal tradition. Scholars called rabbis interpreted the Torah and the *Halacha*. Many of the old Temple rituals were transferred to the synagogues, and regular daily prayers were organized.

The destruction of the Second Temple in Jerusalem by Roman soldiers in 70 CE by 19th-century Italian painter Francesco Hayez. The Temple was never rebuilt.

JERUSALEM

Jerusalem is holy to Jews, Christians and Muslims. It has been the spiritual home of the Jewish people since ancient times. According to biblical accounts, Jerusalem became the capital of Israel under King David and was once again a Jewish capital under the Hasmonean dynasty of the Maccabees, from 164 BCE to the first century CE. During the Jewish rebellion against Roman rule of 66–70 CE, Jerusalem was destroyed. The city came under Christian rule from the fourth to the seventh century, and then Muslim rule for most of the period from the seventh to the 20th century. Nevertheless, Jews around the world maintained their emotional and spiritual attachment to the holy city. In 1949, the newly formed Jewish State of Israel named Jerusalem as its capital.

By the end of the second century CE, the interpretation of the *Halacha* had become increasingly complex. There existed a mass of material concerning various decisions and debates that had taken place, but it was not recorded in an organized fashion. A rabbi named Judah Ha-Nasi (135–c. 220 CE) began compiling the legal decisions so that the Jews would have a code to which they could refer. The result was the Mishnah, a collection of Jewish laws covering a whole range of human activities, including farming, raising taxes, festivals, marriage, crime and ritual purity.

The Middle Ages

In the fourth century CE, Christianity became the official religion of the Roman Empire. The Christian Church was intolerant of Judaism. Christians believed that God had rejected the Jews and had delivered a new message to humankind through Jesus Christ. As far as the Christians were concerned, the Jews had failed to heed the new message and were responsible for Jesus' death. Roman law made it illegal to convert to Judaism and for Christians and Jews to intermarry. From the start of the fifth century CE, Jews were not allowed to hold government positions. By the Middle Ages (500–1500 CE), the Christian Church was dominating most aspects of life and Jews living in Europe often experienced hatred and humiliation. However, life was generally easier for Jews living under Islamic rule in the Middle East, North Africa and Spain.

The Jews under Islam

In the early seventh century, the religion of Islam arose under the leadership of its founder, the Prophet Muhammad. The new faith spread rapidly from its base in the Arabian Peninsula to encompass, by 744, Syria, Palestine, Egypt, Persia (modern-day Iran)

THE TALMUD

In the fourth century CE, rabbis in Palestine put together the Palestinian Talmud. It contained the Mishnah and a record of scholarly discussions about Jewish law, customs and ethics. Similar work was undertaken by rabbis in Babylon, who created the Babylonian Talmud in about 500 CE. According to Jewish law, authority lies with the most recent work, and thus Jews came to regard the Babylonian Talmud as the main source for Jewish law.

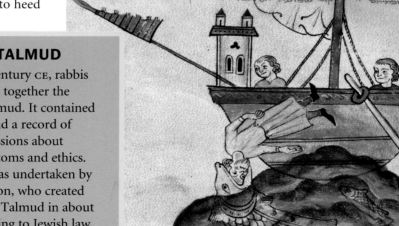

An illustration of Jonah being swallowed by a large fish from the 1299 Cervera Bible. There was a thriving Jewish community in Cervera, a small town in Catalonia, Spain.

The handwritten Hebrew
Talmud scroll.

KARAISM

Karaism was an anti-rabbinic sect
that emerged in the ninth century.
The Karaites based their beliefs
on the ideas of Anan ben David,
an eighth-century Persian Jew.
Ben David's principle was 'search
thoroughly in the Torah and do not
rely on my opinion'. He claimed
that all of Jewish law was contained
in the Torah and that the rabbis' oral
interpretations were unnecessary.
In the ninth century, the Persian
scholar Benjamin ben Moses
Nahawendi established a Karaite sect
in Iran, and the doctrine spread. By
the 11th century, there were Karaites
throughout the Muslim world and
the Byzantine Empire, but by the
late 16th century, the movement
had declined.

and Mesopotamia (modern-day Iraq).
The rulers of this new Islamic empire saw
Christians and Jews as fellow worshippers
of the one true God and allowed them to
practise their faith. Jews were restricted
in certain ways, however. For example,
they had to wear special clothing and pay
an annual tax imposed on non-Muslims.
Yet Jews prospered under Islamic rule,
becoming skilled craftsmen and taking
advantage of the established trading
networks to become successful merchants.

Jewish people ran their own
communities. They established religious
academies called *yeshivot*. The *gaon*,

the head of the *yeshiva*, was the senior
religious authority in the community. He
organized the Jewish courts and appointed
the religious officials, including the ritual
slaughterers who made sure animals were
killed for food according to the Jewish
dietary laws.

**North Africa and Andalusia in the tenth
and eleventh centuries showing the Jewish
cultural centres and the conquests by the
Muslim Almoravid dynasty.**

Scholars, poets and statesmen

Although Jews maintained their separate identity, their culture was influenced by Islamic traditions, and Jewish scholars wrote philosophical and scientific works in Arabic. In North Africa and Al-Andalus (the part of Spain under Muslim rule), Jewish culture blossomed during the 10th and 11th centuries. For example, the Tunisian Jewish scholar Isaac ben Solomon Israeli wrote on medicine and philosophy. In the 10th century, Hasdai ibn Shaprut (c. 915–c. 975) from Córdoba in Al-Andalus was court physician to the Muslim rulers, and a diplomat who helped them to negotiate with the Christian rulers of northern Spain. The poet and philosopher Solomon ibn Gabirol (c. 1022–c. 1058/70) wrote poetry modelled on the Arabic style of the time, but with biblical influences.

This undated engraving shows Jews being expelled from Spain in 1492 by order of the Inquisition. Only Jews who had converted to Christianity were allowed to stay.

KABBALAH

Kabbalah, meaning 'that which is received', is a set of Jewish mystical teachings that originated in ancient times. The early writings describe the journeys of wise men ascending through heavenly palaces to behold God on his throne. Kabbalah reached its height during the Middle Ages in Spain and southern France. A significant work was the late-12th-century *Sefer ha-Bahir* (Book of Brightness), which explains how God created the universe and describes the mystical significance of the shapes and sounds of the Hebrew alphabet. In the 13th century, a school of Kabbalah developed in Gerona, northern Spain. Rabbi Moses de Leon (1250–1305) drew on the teachings of the Gerona school to produce the influential *Sefer ha-Zohar* (Book of Splendour), which explains the inner, mystical meaning of the Torah and teaches that human action in the service of God can help repair disharmony in the world and bring union with God. After the Jews were expelled from Spain in 1492, some made their way to Safed in northern Palestine, which became the principal centre of development for Kabbalah in the 16th century.

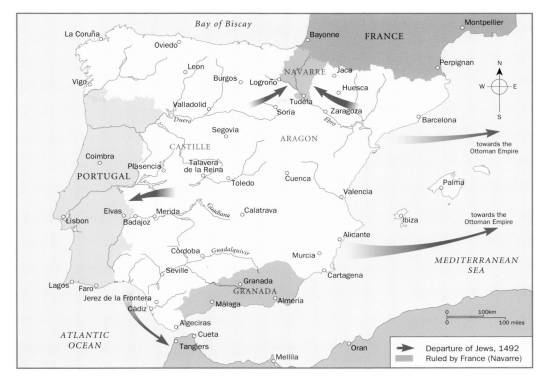

In January 1492, following the fall of Granada, the Christian reconquest of Spain was complete. King Ferdinand and Queen Isabella of Spain ordered all the Jews to leave the country.

Persecution

In 1146, the extreme Muslim Almohad dynasty from North Africa began to conquer Al-Andalus. The Almohads did not allow Jews to follow their religion, closed their *yeshivot* and synagogues and forced them to convert to Islam. Many Jews fled north to the Christian-ruled part of Spain, where Jews were accepted, while others practised their faith in secret. Some escaped to North Africa, including the philosopher Maimonides (1135–1204). Despite the difficulties, this was a period of enormous Jewish creativity. Maimonides produced an important code of Jewish law, the *Mishneh Torah*, while the Jewish mystical work, *Sefer ha-Zohar*, was compiled by Rabbi Moses ben Shem Tov de Leon (1250–1305).

Reconquest

From the 12th century, Christian forces reconquered much of Al-Andalus. At first, Jews fared well under Christian rule, but from the late 14th century onwards they were persecuted. Many Jews were forced to convert to Christianity, but these *conversos* were increasingly regarded with suspicion. In around 1480, the Spanish Inquisition began. This was a court set up by Spain's Christian rulers to put suspected heretics on trial. Thousands of people were convicted of heresy. Their property was confiscated and, in many cases, they were burnt at the stake. In 1492, the Jews were driven out of Spain altogether and they were scattered throughout North Africa, Italy, the Netherlands and the Ottoman Empire.

Jews in Christian Europe

Jews in central and western Europe endured mistrust that regularly turned to violent assault. With the commencement of the Crusades in 1096, religious fervour led to a rise in attacks on Jewish communities. Jews were killed in several towns in the Rhineland area of Germany.

Jews were often accused of monstrous crimes. In 1144, the Jews of Norwich, England, were charged with using the blood of Christian children to make *matzo* (bread made without yeast) for the Jewish festival of Passover. This false accusation, known as the 'blood libel', spread throughout Europe.

Jews were hated not only for religious reasons, but also because of their reputation as moneylenders. Because

This anti-Semitic illustration from around 1478 depicts the common medieval belief that Jewish people used the blood of Christian children in their religious rituals.

they were excluded from numerous professions and trades, many had turned to moneylending, a job forbidden to Christians because they were not allowed to charge interest on loans. Moneylenders were unpopular among the poor, who depended on their services, yet resented being in debt to them.

Laws were introduced that made life harder for European Jews. For instance, in 1215 a Roman Catholic council obliged all Jews in Europe to wear a badge or hat to identify them. During the 14th and 15th centuries, Jews were frequently segregated from the rest of the population; in many towns and cities they were forced to live in ghettos, where they were locked in at night.

Some rulers went so far as to expel their Jewish populations. In 1290, Jews were banished from England. They were forced out of France several times during the 14th century, and regularly expelled from German cities in the 15th and 16th

The Passover Seder salver contains six symbolic items including two types of bitter herbs, a hard-bolied egg, a roasted bone, charoset (a paste of fruits and nuts) and karpas (a vegetable dipped in salt water).

PASSOVER

The Jewish people have kept their history and sense of community alive through their customs. Every year they celebrate the festival of Passover to remember their ancestors' escape from slavery in Egypt. Families gather for the Seder meal on the first evening of the eight-day festival. They carry out rituals that help them to feel connected to their biblical ancestors. They eat matzo, the unleavened bread the Israelites ate during the Exodus, the journey from Egypt. The book read at the Seder is the Haggadah. Since the Middle Ages, it has ended with the phrase 'Next year in Jerusalem', to express the Jewish yearning for their holy land and the long-lost Temple.

centuries. When the Black Death raged through Europe in the mid-14th century, Jews were widely blamed for causing the plague and many were murdered by angry mobs. Poland remained a beacon of tolerance, however; Jews enjoyed protection there from the 13th century.

Jews in Persia Although the Jews were permitted to return to Israel when Persia conquered Babylonia in 538 BCE, many remained in Babylon and spread out around the towns of Babylonia and Persia. In the mid-seventh century, the Arab Muslims conquered Persia, but permitted the Jews to continue practising their religion. However, under the Safavid (1502–1736) and Qajar dynasties (1794–1925) the Jews suffered forced conversion to Islam and many were massacred. Their position then began to gradually improve, until 1979, when a radical Islamic government took power in Iran, leading to an exodus of Iranian Jews.

Jews in Yemen Jews probably arrived in Yemen between the third century BCE and third century CE, although the first evidence of their presence dates from the sixth century CE. Like Jews in other Muslim lands, they were allowed to follow their faith. In the late 19th century, Yemeni Jews began to emigrate to Palestine, and in 1949 and 1950, most of the Jews still remaining in Yemen were brought to the newly established State of Israel.

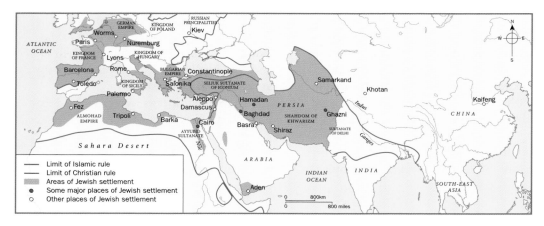

Jews in China There is evidence of a Jewish presence in China from the eighth century CE, although Jews may have arrived much earlier. Kaifeng, in eastern China, had a Jewish community dating from the 11th century, and in 1163 a synagogue was built there. Over the years, the Kaifeng

This map shows the Jewish world in 1200: the Jews were widely dispersed by this time.

Jews dispersed or assimilated and lost their Jewish identity. Modern Jewish communities formed again during the 19th and 20th centuries. The greatest numbers came as refugees during World War II, but most dispersed to other countries after the war.

MATTEO RICCI AND THE KAIFENG JEWS

The Italian Jesuit priest and missionary Matteo Ricci (1552–1610) related in his letters how he discovered the Jews of China through an interesting encounter. In 1605, a Kaifeng Jew named Ai Tien was called to a meeting with Ricci at his home in Beijing. He had heard that, unlike the Chinese, Ricci believed in one God. Ai Tien thought that Ricci must be a Jewish rabbi, while Ricci believed Ai Tien to be a Christian. The pair looked at a painting together. Ai Tien thought it showed four of the twelve sons of Jacob and was surprised to learn they were the four Apostles of Christ. He asked who Christ was. Ricci realized that Ai Tien was in fact Jewish, not Christian, and he told him about Christianity.

Jews in India The largest group of Indian Jews, the Bene Israel, claimed to have migrated to India from Palestine in the second century BCE, although there is no actual evidence of this. It is more likely that Jews came to India from Spain, Portugal, Persia, Afghanistan and Mesopotamia during the 16th and 17th centuries.

Although they followed a similar lifestyle in many ways to their Hindu and Muslim neighbours, the Bene Israel also practised Jewish customs such as circumcision, and observed the Sabbath and kosher food laws. The Jewish communities maintained their independence when India was under British rule (1858–1947), but most moved to Israel after its establishment in 1948.

Jews in Ethiopia Jewish Ethiopians call themselves Beta Esrael but are also known as Falashas. According to their tradition, they came to Ethiopia after the Exodus from Egypt or after the destruction of the First Temple. Little is known about their history before the 13th century, but between the 13th and 15th centuries, the Beta Esrael struggled against Muslim and Christian rulers to retain their independence. They continued to survive on the margins of Ethiopian society until the 20th century. The State of Israel did not accept them as Jews at first – they were not recognized as such until 1973. Most Beta Esrael were evacuated to Israel in air-rescue operations, first during a famine in 1984 and then again during political unrest in 1991.

Sephardim During the Middle Ages the majority of Jews were concentrated in Spain and the Islamic countries, and in northern and eastern Europe. The Jews expelled from Spain in 1492 (and from Portugal in 1497) mainly migrated to the Muslim Ottoman Empire in North Africa and the Middle East. They became known as Sephardim (Spanish).

The Sephardic Jews were permitted to follow their faith in the Ottoman Empire as long as they accepted Muslim rule and paid the tax on non-Muslims. A distinctive Sephardic culture developed. They spoke their own language, called Ladino, which included Spanish and Hebrew words. The Sephardic Jews prospered under Ottoman rule. They set up the empire's first printing press in 1493, and Jewish literature flourished. Most court physicians were Jews, as were many diplomats.

Ethiopian Jews gather outside the Israeli Embassy in the Ethiopian capital Addis Ababa in 1991 as they prepare to leave the country. They were airlifted to Israel during Operation Solomon.

Ashkenazim The Jews forced out of Germany in the 15th and 16th centuries settled in Poland, and became known as Ashkenazim (Germans). They spoke their own dialect, Yiddish, which contained elements of German and Hebrew, and played eastern European music. Most Jews lived in their own *shtetls* (villages), with synagogues and *yeshivot*.

Poland and Lithuania became centres of Jewish cultural life. For example, the Jeshybot Yeshiva, established in Lublin, Poland, in 1515, became an important centre for Talmudic study. Rabbi Moses Isserles, who helped write the *Shulkhan Arukh*, studied there, and the city became known as the 'Jewish Oxford'. Because of their emphasis on religious study, the Jewish people enjoyed a higher standard of literacy than their Christian neighbours. Although they suffered some discrimination, such as having to wear

This map indicates the main migrations of Jewish communities to the Ottoman Empire in the 15th and 16th centuries. At the end of the 15th century, around 20,000 Jews who had been expelled from Spain went to Salonika (modern-day Thessaloníki, in Greece).

SEPHARDIC AND ASHKENAZIC PRACTICES

Sephardic and Ashkenazic Jews both use Hebrew as their language of worship. They read the same Torah and Talmud, say the same prayers, eat kosher food and celebrate the same festivals. Yet they have separate synagogues because they have different traditions of worship. For example, Sephardim use their own poems and psalms in their services. They chant the Torah in a different way from Ashkenazim and sing prayers to different melodies.

In 1565, Sephardic rabbi Joseph Caro published a legal code for Sephardic Judaism called the *Shulkhan Arukh*. In 1570–1571, it was reissued with modifications by Rabbi Moses Isserles to include Ashkenazic customs. Thus, guidance for the religious behaviour of both communities was unified in a single book. Nevertheless, the two traditions maintained their separate practices.

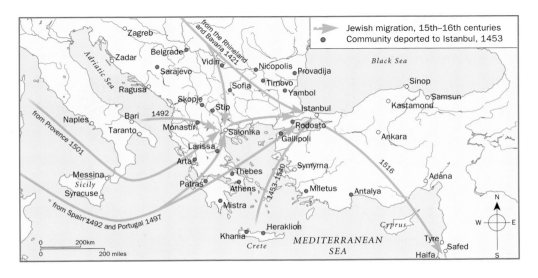

distinctive clothing, Jews were allowed to run their own communities. Many found employment working for the nobility, running their estates and collecting taxes from the peasantry.

However, anti-Jewish hatred grew in Poland during the 17th century. In 1648, the Cossacks, a Ukrainian people living under Polish authority, rebelled against the Polish nobility. Led by Bogdan Chmielnicki, they punished the Jews because they worked for the nobles. It is estimated that a quarter of the Jewish community in Poland died in a frenzy of torture and massacre, while others were sold into slavery. The Jews were subsequently attacked by the Russians, who were allied with Chmielnicki. When the Swedes invaded western Poland, Jewish people were assaulted by Poles who believed the Jews had encouraged the invasion. The Cossacks committed further violence against the Jews in the 18th century, when Poland was partitioned. By 1795, the Jewish population was split between Russia, Prussia and Austria.

Religious movements

A new Jewish movement arose in Poland during the struggles of the 18th century, founded by Rabbi Israel ben Eliezer (1698–1760), also known as the Baal Shem Tov (Master of the Good Name), or the Besht. The movement was based on a joyful worship of God under the guidance of a *tzaddik* (spiritual leader). The followers of the Besht were known as the Hasidim (Pious Ones), and after his death the Hasidic movement spread throughout Poland and eastern Europe.

When the Hasidic movement reached Lithuania in the late 18th century, it was resisted fiercely. Rabbi Elijah ben Solomon Zalman (1720–1797), the *gaon* of the city of Vilna, established a movement in opposition to the Hasidim, the Mitnaggdim (Opponents). The Mitnaggdim defended traditional values, including the intensive study of the Torah and Talmud, and rejected the honouring of *tzaddikim* (spiritual leaders). Both movements ran *yeshivot* that taught their own doctrines.

Hasidic Jews in modern-day Jaffa, Israel, in their typical clothing. The movement spread to the USA in the late 19th century, where the majority of followers currently live.

From the late 16th century, western European countries that had previously expelled Jews began to allow them to return. In 1670, the ruler of Brandenburg, Germany, invited Jews to settle because they were skilled traders and could help revive the economy after the Thirty Years' War (1618–1648). Around the same time, Jews were permitted to return to France. Yet Jews were still barred from many occupations, and craft and trade guilds. In England, Jews could neither hold public office nor attend university. Towards the end of the 18th century, some of the restrictions were lifted in central Europe, and in France Jews were granted full civil rights after the revolution of 1789. During the 19th century, equal rights were given to all Jewish people in Europe, except for those living in the Russian Empire.

Samson Raphael Hirsch did not believe that Judaism should be changed:

Was Judaism ever 'in accordance with the times'? Did Judaism ever correspond with the views of dominant contemporaries? Was it ever convenient to be a Jew or a Jewess?… Was that Judaism in accordance with the times, for which, during the centuries following the Dispersion, our fathers suffered in all lands, through all the various periods, the most degrading oppression, the most biting contempt, and a thousand-fold death and persecution? And yet we would make it the aim and scope of Judaism to be always 'in accordance with the times'!

The Nineteen Letters on Judaism, 1836.
From Louis Jacobs. Oxford University Press (1995); myjewishlearning.com.

The Jewish Enlightenment

The Enlightenment was an 18th-century movement in western Europe that emphasized reason and science in the study of the human and natural world. Jewish thinkers in the late 18th and early 19th centuries applied these principles to their religion and founded a Jewish Enlightenment, known as the Haskalah. The most influential of these thinkers, Moses Mendelssohn (1729–1786) from Berlin, Germany, believed that Jews should try to fit in better with the society around them. They should study secular (non-religious) as well as religious subjects and learn the language of their adopted

At this Yom Kippur service in a Reform synagogue, there is no separation between men and women.

This map shows the European countries that emancipated the Jews – freeing them from legal, social and political restrictions – along with the date of their emancipation.

country. His followers were known as the *maskilim*. They laid the foundations for the Reform movement.

The Reform movement

Israel Jacobson (1768–1828) founded the Reform movement in Germany. He set up schools where Jewish children learnt secular as well as religious subjects. The movement attempted to adapt the Jewish religion to the conditions of the modern world and make it easier for Jews to be full citizens of their country. Reform synagogue services were in German rather than Hebrew, and men and women – traditionally seated apart – sat together. Work was permitted on the Sabbath, and people no longer had to follow the kosher food laws.

Many Jews feared that these changes would lead to assimilation. A division grew between Reform and Orthodox Jews. In Germany, the most prominent Orthodox thinker was Samson Raphael Hirsch (1808–1888). Hirsch believed that Jews should stick to traditional practices, but he accepted that they could have a secular education as well. This type of thinking became known as neo-Orthodoxy.

Some Orthodox Jews opposed all changes to Judaism. Rabbi Moses Sofer (1762–1839) challenged the Reform movement in early 19th-century Germany. His motto was: 'Anything new is forbidden by the Torah.' His views influenced the development of Haredi Judaism (see page 35).

Anti-Semitism In the late 19th century, nationalism was on the rise in Europe. Nations were developing a strong sense of national identity based on the dominant ethnic group in their society. Minority groups with their own customs, especially the Jews, were seen as outsiders posing a threat to social cohesion. The increasing presence of Jews in mainstream society – in the professions, finance and the arts – was resented, as was their growing wealth and economic power. A modern form of anti-Semitism emerged, based on so-called 'racial' rather than religious differences. Many believed that the Jews were a sinister race that wanted to dominate the world.

Anti-Semitism became widespread in Germany and France. In 1880s Russia, new restrictions were placed on where Jews could settle, and strict quotas were imposed to limit the number of Jews in the professions and universities. Of the anti-Semitic works published the best known was the *Protocols of the Elders of Zion*, first published in Russia in 1903. Apparently written by a secret Jewish organization determined to achieve world domination, it was in fact a forgery. Between 1881 and 1921, Jewish communities in Russia and other parts of eastern Europe suffered waves of pogroms – outbreaks of anti-Semitic violence, including murder, rape and the destruction of property.

Zionism Jewish people reacted in various ways to the devastating attacks. A minority were drawn to the Zionist movement, founded by an Austro-Hungarian Jewish journalist and political activist, Theodor Herzl. Herzl came to believe that anti-Semitism would always exist and that the only solution was to establish a Jewish state in the historic land of Israel. In 1897, he founded the World Zionist Organization. Few Jews were living in Palestine at the time, but the pogroms in eastern Europe led to increased Jewish emigration there.

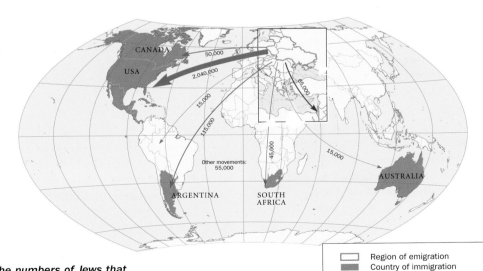

The numbers of Jews that emigrated from eastern Europe between 1881 and 1914 and the countries to which they moved.

An assault on Jews in Kiev in the Russian Empire during the 1880s. The police look on and do nothing to stop the violence.

Migration

The majority of Jews who emigrated from Europe to escape persecution went to the USA rather than Palestine. Between 1881 and 1914, about two million eastern European Jews moved to the United States. Others moved to western Europe, South Africa, Argentina and Canada. Most of the Jewish immigrants arriving in their host countries were deeply religious and very poor. By contrast, existing Jewish communities tended to be quite assimilated. Immigrants often found it hard to adjust to their new situation. In Britain, for example, non-Jewish employers expected Jews to work on the Sabbath. Within a couple of generations, however, the immigrants had adapted to life within their adopted countries.

Socialism

Some Jewish people reacted to anti-Semitism by joining revolutionary socialist movements. As a persecuted people, Jews were attracted to the radical idea of an equal society.

In this excerpt from Theodor Herzl's 1896 book *The Jewish State*, he outlines his view of anti-Semitism:

The Jewish question exists wherever Jews live in perceptible numbers. Where it does not exist, it is carried by Jews in the course of their migrations. We naturally move to those places where we are not persecuted, and there our presence produces persecution. This is the case in every country, and will remain … until the Jewish question finds a solution on a political basis. The unfortunate Jews are now carrying the seeds of Anti-Semitism into England; they have already introduced it into America.

Rather than emigrating or establishing a Jewish state, socialist Jews believed they should struggle alongside other workers to overthrow existing governments. In 1897, Jewish workers established the Bund – the General Union of Jewish Workers in Lithuania, Poland and Russia. Jewish people, such as Leon Trotsky, played a prominent role in the 1917 Russian Revolution, while Rosa Luxemburg, was one of the leaders of the 1918–19 socialist uprising in Germany.

The revolutionary Bolshevik government in Russia overturned the laws against Jews, but was also committed to the abolition of religion. As part of a campaign against religious practices, in 1918 many Jewish organizations were closed down, and it was forbidden to teach Hebrew. The anti-capitalist Bolsheviks also closed down the small businesses on which many Jews relied for a living and pushed Jewish people into jobs in agriculture and heavy industry.

World War I In 1914, war broke out between the major European powers. At this time, around four million Jews were living on the war's Eastern Front, where Russia was fighting Germany and Austria-Hungary. The Russian government suspected that Jews were collaborating with the enemy and deported them from the region, testing Jewish loyalty to Russia severely. Nevertheless, around half a million Jews joined the Russian army.

The USA was the most popular destination for Jewish emigrants from all eastern European countries. This map gives the numbers who left between 1899 and 1914.

WELFARE ORGANIZATIONS IN THE USA

Throughout history, Jews had always supported the less fortunate in their community. It was an obligation within Jewish law to help the needy by putting donations in the *kuppah*, or collection box. The funds were distributed to good causes, ranging from soup kitchens to burial societies. When penniless eastern European Jews arrived in the United States, this system continued. Jewish welfare organizations were established in several American cities. As well as providing health care and housing for the elderly, they opened Jewish community centres, which offered cultural, educational and recreational activities.

In other lands, large numbers of Jews also fought for their country – nearly 100,000 in Germany, for example. Yet hostility towards them continued. They were accused of avoiding army service

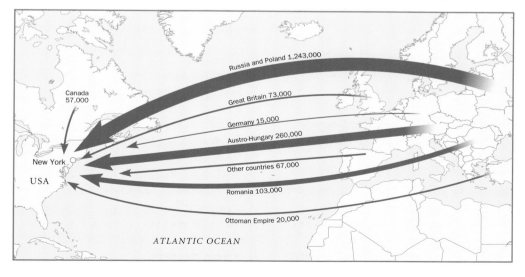

Russia and Poland 1,243,000
Canada 57,000
Great Britain 73,000
Germany 15,000
Austro-Hungary 260,000
New York
Other countries 67,000
USA
Romania 103,000
Ottoman Empire 20,000
ATLANTIC OCEAN

and of profiteering. In the USA and Britain, Jews were suspected of supporting Germany because of their hostility towards Russia. Jews of German origin were forced to sign a declaration of loyalty to their host country. After the war ended in 1918, German Jews were blamed for their country's defeat.

Zionism gathers pace
In 1918, the British captured Palestine from the collapsing Ottoman Empire, and, two years later, Britain established a mandate over the country. In the Balfour Declaration of 1917, Britain had expressed support for the establishment of a Jewish homeland in Palestine. This declaration encouraged the Zionists, and Jewish emigration to Palestine increased. The Jewish community grew from 90,000 at the end of World War I to about 160,000 in 1929, and nearly 500,000 by 1939.

The Palestinian community resented the influx of settlers. In 1921, the Jewish National Fund bought up Arab land for Jewish settlement, and Arab peasants were evicted, leading to anti-Zionist riots. Several Arab organizations protested to the British about Jewish immigration, and there were further riots in 1929, and a widespread rebellion took place between 1936 and 1939. It proved impossible to reconcile the interests of the Zionists and the Palestinians.

The rise of Nazism
In the early 1930s, Europe and the USA were hit by a severe economic depression. Germany was hit especially hard. The government was in crisis and looked to a strong leader. In 1933, Nazi leader Adolf Hitler was appointed chancellor of Germany. Hitler blamed the Jews and Communists for Germany's economic problems. Between

A man clears up the broken glass in a Jewish-owned shop after it was damaged during **Kristallnacht***, November 1938. The Nazis had ordered the police and fire services not to interfere with the attacks unless non-Jewish property was threatened with damage.*

1933 and 1939, he brought in a series of anti-Jewish laws. German Jews were deprived of citizenship, lost their jobs in the professions and soon all their freedoms. In 1938, during an organized Nazi attack that became known as *Kristallnacht* (the Night of Broken Glass), hundreds of synagogues in Germany and Austria were burnt to the ground, thousands of Jewish businesses were destroyed, and at least 35 Jews were murdered.

THE WARSAW GHETTO UPRISING

Despite the overwhelming power of the Nazis, Jewish people opposed them where they could. Some joined the Allied war effort or partisan groups; others resisted through armed struggle. The most significant revolt took place in the Warsaw Ghetto in Poland. In July 1942, the Nazis began deporting Jews from the ghetto, sending two-thirds of the 300,000 inhabitants to the death camps. In January 1943, Nazi troops surrounded the ghetto, ready to send all the remaining inhabitants for extermination. The Jewish ghetto fighters mounted a heroic defence, forcing the Nazis to fight the biggest battle on Polish soil since German occupation of the country in 1939. The majority of the resistance fighters died in action, and the Nazis managed to crush the uprising in May 1943.

After Hitler gained power, Jewish people left Germany if they could. However, the USA and Europe, which were still in the throes of economic depression, were accepting few immigrants. In an attempt to pacify the Palestinians, the British restricted Jewish immigration to Palestine, too.

After World War II broke out in 1939, Nazi Germany conquered a vast swathe of Europe, imposing anti-Semitic laws on defeated populations. Many Jews were deported to Poland and forced to do hard labour for the Nazis. International Jewish organizations such as the Joint Distribution Committee rescued some German Jews and helped them to reach safe countries.

The Holocaust In 1941, Germany invaded the Soviet Union. Special German troops called the *Einsatzgruppen* rounded up Jews and Communists and murdered them. Later that year, the Nazis started to build death camps in occupied Poland. Jews from Nazi-occupied countries were transported to the camps in cattle trucks. The young and fit were made to work, while the rest were killed in gas chambers. It is estimated that between 1941 and 1945, six million Jews were murdered, starved, beaten or worked to death. This attempt to wipe out the entire Jewish population of Europe became known as the Holocaust.

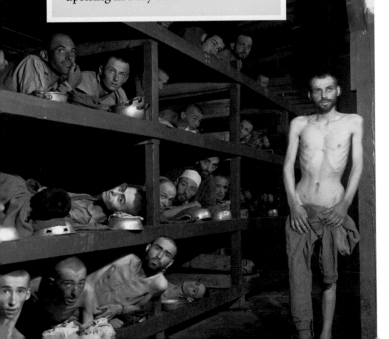

In April 1945, the Allies liberated Buchenwald concentration camp. Most of the survivors were very ill and starving. Only a minority of European Jews escaped the Nazis' efforts to wipe out an entire people.

Few nations helped the Jews, although some courageous individuals risked their lives to save Jewish people. For instance, in 1943, the Nazis planned to deport Danish Jews to death camps, but members of the Danish resistance movement shipped them to safety in Sweden, which was not involved in the war. Yet by the end of the war in 1945, about 70 per cent of Europe's Jews were dead, and the Jewish culture of eastern Europe had been virtually destroyed.

Jewish survivors of the war were in a desperate situation. Some tried to return to their home countries, but most found themselves in Displaced Persons' (DP) camps in Germany and Austria. A minority were permitted to enter the USA, but in 1947, 300,000 Jews were still in DP camps.

The horrors of the Holocaust provoked a worldwide outpouring of sympathy for the Jewish people, giving fresh impetus to the Zionist project. Although it was illegal for large numbers to enter Palestine, around 69,000 homeless Jews attempted to move there. The British could no longer cope with the tensions between the Palestinians and Jews and announced their desire to end their mandate in May 1948. The United Nations (UN) was called upon to try to resolve the conflict.

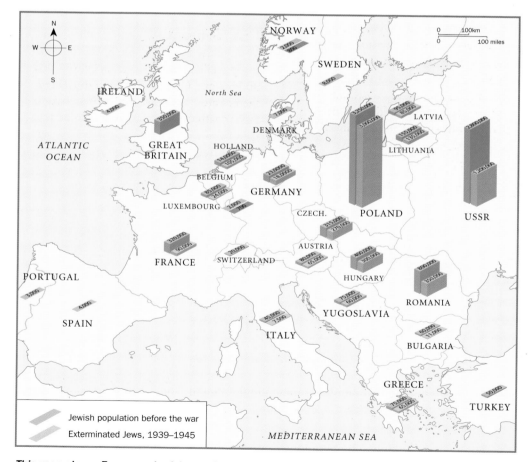

This map shows European Jewish populations before the start of World War II in 1939, and in 1945, after the Holocaust. The largest and oldest Jewish communities in the world were destroyed.

The State of Israel

The UN voted to divide the country between the Jews and the Palestinians, but the Palestinians did not agree to the partition plan, and fighting eventually broke out between the two nations. In May 1948, the State of Israel was declared. The day after the declaration, the armies of neighbouring pro-Palestinian Arab states – Egypt, Transjordan, Iraq, Syria and Lebanon – invaded Israel, starting a war that didn't end until January 1949.

Under the final armistice agreement of July 1949, Israel secured over 77 per cent of former Palestine territory – 22 per cent more than it had been offered under the UN plan. Transjordan took over East Jerusalem and the West Bank, and Egypt occupied the Gaza Strip. Thus, the State of Israel did not include the entire area of the ancient land of Israel, but it did include the holy cities of Safed and Tiberias, and the western part of Jerusalem. The Palestinians, however, were allocated no land, and around 726,000 of them were forced out or fled the country as refugees.

Between 1948 and 1951, the population of Israel expanded rapidly with the arrival of 688,000 immigrants. Several thousand arrived from the DP camps of Europe. Jews also came from Muslim countries, where sympathy with the Palestinians had led to anti-Semitism. Absorbing the immigrants was a huge challenge for the new state. America provided support, and donations came in from Jews around the world, supplemented by the reparations (compensation for war crimes) paid by Germany.

However, the new Jewish homeland did not enjoy peace. There was continual tension between Israel and its Arab neighbours who did not accept the Jewish state, and Israel was determined to defend itself against them. Meanwhile, up to 460,000 Palestinians remained in refugee camps in the West Bank and Gaza Strip, desperate to return to their homes within Israel.

Jewish territory on the eve of independence
Territory acquired by Israel 1948–49
Armistice line 1949
Arab countries

LEBANON
Tyre
Metullah
SYRIA
Safed
Acre
Galilee
Haifa
Sea of Galilee
Tiberias
Jezreel Valley
Nazareth
Beth-Shean
Hadera
Jenin
Netanya
Tul Karm
MEDITERRANEAN SEA
Qalqilya
Nablus
Tel Aviv
Petah Tikvah
Jaffa
WEST BANK
Lod
Ramla
Ramallah
Yavneh
Jericho
Ashdod
Jerusalem
Dead Sea
Gaza
Hebron
GAZA STRIP
Ruhamah
Tekumah
Beersheba
Gevulot
Sedom
Haluza
TRANSJORDAN
Negev Desert
EGYPT

0 50km
0 50 miles

N
W E
S

Eilat

This map shows the territory gained by Israel during the war of 1948–1949 and the borders defined by the armistice agreements of 1949.

Israel expands

During the Arab-Israeli War of 1967, Israel conquered East Jerusalem, the West Bank and the Gaza Strip. The Jewish state now ruled a large part of historic Israel, including significant Jewish holy sites such as the holy city of Hebron and the Western Wall in Jerusalem – all that remains of the Second Temple after its destruction in 70 CE (see page 12). Throughout history, Jews have expressed grief at the destruction of the Temple and have prayed for it to be restored. The site of the Temple is called the Temple Mount. It also includes significant Muslim holy sites – the Dome of the Rock and the Al-Aqsa Mosque. Since Israel took control of the area in 1967, there have been disputes with Palestinian Muslims over control and access to the sacred site.

DAVID BEN-GURION
(1886–1973)

As a young man in Poland, David Ben-Gurion was a committed Zionist. He emigrated to Palestine at the age of 20, but when World War I broke out he was expelled from the country for his Zionist activities (Palestine was then ruled by the Ottoman Empire). He returned to Palestine when the British took control. Ben-Gurion founded the Histadrut, the Jewish workers' trade union in 1920, and the Israeli Workers' Party in 1930. In 1935, he was elected chairman of the Zionist Executive, which led world Zionism. When Britain restricted immigration to Palestine in 1939, Ben-Gurion called on the Zionists to fight the British and make Palestine impossible to govern, in order to help achieve a Jewish state. In May 1948, he became the first prime minister of Israel.

David Ben-Gurion reads out the Declaration of Independence at the Tel Aviv Museum; above him is a portrait of Theodor Herzl. The USA was the first country to recognize Israel.

JEWS IN THE SOVIET UNION

In the Soviet Union, religious practice was discouraged and quotas restricted the number of Jews allowed to go to university and to enter the professions. Jewish history and religious studies had to be taught in secret. Like all citizens of the Soviet Union, Jews were not permitted to leave the country, although after 1968 the rules were gradually relaxed and Jews were allowed to emigrate to Israel. About 300,000 Jews left between 1969 and 1989. However, many did not want to live in Israel and subsequently made their way to the USA. Following the fall of the Soviet Union in 1990, around one million Soviet Jews emigrated to Israel.

Further wars took place between Israel and the neighbouring Arab countries in 1973 and 1982, as well as Palestinian uprisings against Israeli occupation from 1987 to 1993 and from 2000 to 2005. Israel has fought intermittent wars with the militant groups Hamas (in Gaza) and Hezbollah (in southern Lebanon) since 2006. Since the 1970s, there have also been efforts at peace: Israel signed a peace treaty with Egypt in 1979 and with Jordan in 1994. In 2005, Israel withdrew its armed forces and settlers from Gaza. Yet the core conflict between Israel and the Palestinians over the land of former Palestine, and how to share it, remains unresolved.

The conflict is essentially a political problem with religious dimensions. While the majority of Israeli citizens are Jewish, the majority of the population of the

Israeli soldiers after the capture of the Western Wall in East Jerusalem during the 1967 Arab-Israeli war. The Palestinians hoped that East Jerusalem could be the capital of a future Palestinian state, yet Israel would be unwilling to give up control over it.

West Bank and Gaza Strip are Muslims. How can Israel retain its Jewish nature if a large part of the population under its rule is non-Jewish? Owing to the higher birth rate of Muslim Palestinians compared with Jews, many Israelis are concerned that Palestinians could become the majority in the State of Israel within 30 or 40 years. On the other hand, how can Israel be truly democratic while the Palestinians in the West Bank remain under the military control of Israel and do not enjoy equal rights with Israelis? Even Palestinians within Israel, although they are citizens of the state, suffer from discrimination in many areas of life.

Judaism in Israel Jews make up around four-fifths of Israel's population – the majority of the other fifth are Muslim Palestinians. The main groups of Jews are Ashkenazim from central and eastern Europe and Sephardim from the Mediterranean region and North Africa. There are also Jews from western Europe, Central Asia, and North and South America.

Jews in Israel tend to define themselves as either religious or non-religious rather than identifying themselves with a specific denomination. Among the non-religious are the secular Jews, who are mostly Ashkenazim. Others,

mainly Sephardim, consider themselves traditionalists. They are committed to Judaism but do not carry out all the religious rituals. Non-religious Jews do take part in some Jewish customs to varying degrees. For example, most attend a Seder at Passover. Many Israeli Jews feel they are expressing their Judaism sufficiently simply by living in Israel, and they don't need to carry out religious rituals as well.

Those who describe themselves as religious are Orthodox, a term that covers a wide spectrum of religious practice. The most Orthodox are the Haredi Jews. They follow the traditions laid down in the written Torah, along with the Talmud, the earliest written form of the *Halacha*. They adopt an extremely modest dress code and live in their own separate community.

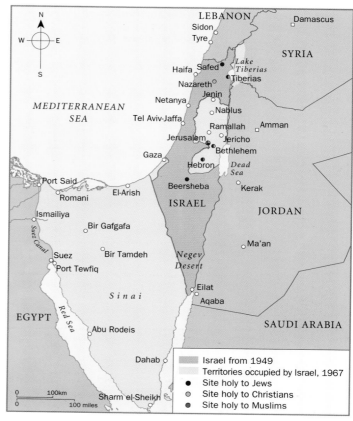

This map shows the territory gained by Israel in the 1967 war as well as the holy sites in the country.

Judaism in the diaspora

Within the diaspora, there is a wide variety of religious practice. Many Jews are secular or completely assimilated into the majority culture. The movements within modern Judaism range from the most Orthodox through the Conservative and Reform movements to the Reconstructionists. The term Orthodox covers all those who observe the traditional practices of Judaism strictly. Orthodox Jews form the largest movement in the UK.

Founded in the USA in the early 20th century, the Conservative movement is based on the belief that the truths of the Jewish scriptures come from God, but were transmitted by people. Conservative Jews accept the *Halacha* but believe that it should be flexible and adapt to changing circumstances while staying true to Jewish values. The movement is committed to supporting Israel; many Conservative Jews feel that Jewish nationalism is a vital part of their culture. In the UK, it is known as the Masorti movement.

Reform Judaism is the largest Jewish movement in the USA. Reform Jews accept that all Jewish people should study their traditions and carry out the *mitzvoth* that are relevant to modern society. They believe that their religion has evolved over time and will continue to do so. Each individual has the right to decide whether to adopt a particular belief or practice.

THE MESSIAH

There is a traditional Jewish belief that one day the Messiah will come, a man who will rebuild the Temple in Jerusalem, gather all the Jews to Israel and unite all people in the knowledge of the God of Israel. He will end all hatred, disease and suffering and bring world peace: *Nation shall not lift up sword against nation, neither shall man learn war anymore.*

Isaiah 2:4

Jewish families keep their traditions alive by celebrating the Passover Seder, when they remember the Jews' escape from Egypt.

Sephardic Jews from Morocco at a festival to honour the Jewish philosopher Maimonides. The Sephardic and Ashkenazic communities in Israel each have their own chief rabbi.

In many ways the most radical is the Reconstructionist movement, founded in the USA in 1922. Reconstructionists believe that Judaism is a culture that was developed by human beings. They do not believe that the Torah is the word of God. Jewish people should maintain their culture and identity by carrying out religious rituals and learning their history. But they should mix freely with other people and work to promote values of freedom and justice. Reconstructionists support Israel as the focus for the Jewish people in a similar way to Conservative Jews.

The future Some people believe that the future of Judaism is bleak. The religious community is split. Orthodox Jews do not accept the other traditions as valid, while most Reform and Conservative Jews do not believe that the Torah is God's word. The number of Jews worldwide is declining, and many are marrying non-Jews and assimilating into mainstream society. Eventually, Jewish traditions are likely to disappear.

Others argue that Judaism has always adapted to new situations. Although religious observance is declining, sufficient numbers will remain faithful to the Torah and the synagogue. Many secular Jews retain their Jewish identity and links with the community. Although Judaism is fragmented, it will nevertheless survive as a major world faith.

RELIGIOUS LAWS IN ISRAEL

Religion affects how Israel is governed. For example:
- Kosher food is provided in the army and all government institutions.
- It is illegal to import non-kosher foods. However, although pig meat is not kosher, there are some Israeli pork farms; this meat is particularly popular among Russian immigrants.
- Jewish law governs marriage and divorce – it is not possible to have a civil wedding.
- Most businesses close on the Jewish Sabbath (Saturday), and there is no public transport on that day.
- The Law of Return (passed in 1950) allows any Jew from around the world to emigrate to Israel.

CHAPTER 2
CHRISTIANITY

THE Christian religion began with the life of Jesus of Nazareth in the first century CE. Christians believe that Jesus is the son of God, and that he came to Earth to save people from their sins and to show them how to live holy lives, following God's commandments. Jesus spent all his life in Palestine in the Middle East. Christians often call the region where he lived the Holy Land. Most of this area is now in the modern state of Israel. Jesus was born around the year 4 CE in the kingdom of Judea. This was the ancient land of the Jews, but by the time of Jesus' birth, it was part of the Roman Empire, governed by King Herod, a local ruler appointed by the Romans to run Judea according to their laws.

The birth of Jesus

The story of Jesus' birth is told in the Bible's New Testament. It begins with the Annunciation, when the Angel Gabriel appeared to a woman named Mary (known to Christians as the Virgin Mary) at her home in the village of Nazareth, in Galilee, a northern region of Palestine. The angel told her she would give birth to the Son of God.

The Roman emperor Augustus had decreed that everyone in the empire must return to their birthplace in order to be registered for a census. Therefore, just before Jesus was born, Mary and her husband Joseph set off on a journey to Joseph's home town of Bethlehem, around 160 kilometres south of Nazareth. The Bible relates how Jesus was born there in a stable, because all the inns in the town were full.

According to the Bible, shortly after Jesus was born, three wise men arrived to worship him. They had travelled from countries in the East, following a very bright star. However, before they reached Bethlehem, the wise men visited King Herod in Jerusalem to ask about the newborn king. Herod felt threatened by this news and tried to kill Jesus by ordering the death of all the baby boys in his kingdom. But Joseph was warned by an angel in a dream, and he escaped with his family to Egypt. Known as the 'flight into Egypt' by the Christians, this long and arduous journey involved crossing the Negev and Sinai deserts.

According to the Bible, the first people to visit the baby Jesus were local shepherds. They were told about his birth by an angel and brought lambs as gifts. This painting, the Adoration of the Shepherds, *is by the 17th-century Spanish artist, Bartolomé Murillo.*

The life of Jesus Jesus and his family stayed in Egypt until Herod died and it was safe to return to Nazareth, where Joseph taught him the trade of carpentry. Jesus spent his childhood in

THE NEW TESTAMENT

The New Testament of the Bible describes the life of Jesus and how his followers went on to spread the Christian faith. The first four books of the New Testament, by the Apostles Matthew, Mark, Luke and John, are known as the Gospels. They were written several decades after Jesus' death with the intention of encouraging faith in Jesus as the son of God. Each of them tells a slightly different version of the story of his life and ministry.

the town, although little else is known about his early years. However, the Gospel of Luke recounts that a 12-year-old Jesus accompanied his parents on a pilgrimage to Jerusalem, where he became separated from them. He was found several days later in a temple discussing religious matters with some of the city's elders.

It is believed that he began his ministry aged around 30 when he was baptized by a preacher named John the Baptist. Jesus then spent 40 days and nights in the harsh, rocky wilderness of Judea, to the south of Jerusalem. According to the Gospels, the Devil tempted Jesus three times, once to turn

stone to bread, once to cast himself off a mountain where angels would save him, and once to offer him all the kingdoms of the world. However, Jesus refused all these temptations and every year Christians remember his time in the wilderness in the season of Lent, which lasts 40 days and immediately precedes Easter.

Most of the events in Jesus' adult life took place around the Sea of Galilee, a large lake on the River Jordan. Jesus travelled from place to place in this area, teaching, healing the sick and performing miracles, and began to attract disciples.

A map of Palestine showing some of the places where Jesus preached. Jesus spent most of his time around the Sea of Galilee, but he also travelled as far north as Sidon and as far south as Bethany.

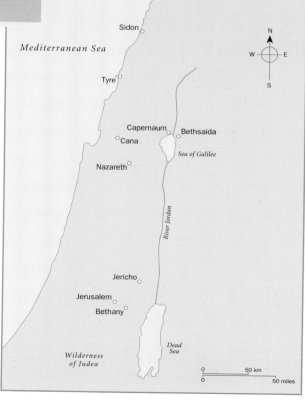

Ministry According to the Gospels, Jesus called his first disciples to leave their fishing nets behind on the banks of the Sea of Galilee, and to follow him. He performed several miracles at the lake. St Matthew tells how he called on a storm to cease and how he walked across its waters on its shores, at Bethsaida, he turned five loaves and two fishes into enough food to feed a crowd of 5,000 people. In Capernaum, on the lake's northern shore, Jesus performed several miracle cures, while further to the west, in the town of Cana, he turned water into wine at a wedding feast.

Jesus preached wherever he went. His most famous lesson was the Sermon on the Mount, ethical teaching based on the law of love. Archaeologists believe that this took place on a hill close to Capernaum, overlooking the Sea of Galilee, known today as the Mount of the Beatitudes.

THE LAST SUPPER

Not long before he was arrested, Jesus shared a special meal with all his disciples. This meal, known as the Last Supper, was held in the upper room of a house in Jerusalem. It was at this last meal that Jesus taught his followers to share bread and wine in memory of him, explaining that they symbolized his body and blood. This was the start of the service of Holy Communion, practised by all Christians, and also known as the Eucharist and the Mass.

The Bible describes several journeys that Jesus undertook with his disciples. He travelled as far north as the ports of Tyre and Sidon, and as far south as Jerusalem. Jesus also spent some time in Bethany, a village close to Jerusalem. This was the home of his friends Mary and Martha and their brother Lazarus. The Gospel of St John tells how Lazarus fell ill and died and then Jesus miraculously brought brought him back to life.

Mount of Olives

City gate

Garden of Gethsemane

The Temple

Hill of Calvary

City wall

Herod's Palace

Probable site of the upper room where the Last Supper was held

A plan of Jerusalem showing some of the places associated with the last few weeks of Jesus' life.

Wherever Jesus travelled, he performed miracles and attracted many followers. Here, Jesus is shown outside the Temple in Jerusalem, curing a man of his disability, while the temple priests look on suspiciously.

In the last weeks of his life, Jesus travelled to Jerusalem. As he drew near the Mount of Olives, a ridge to the east of the city, he sent two disciples to find a donkey, so that he could ride into Jerusalem. As he entered the city, people welcomed him, singing songs and cutting down branches from palm trees to lay in his path.

Arrest For the next few weeks, Jesus preached in Jerusalem and cured the sick. People flocked to see him, praising him as the Son of God. The chief priests, fearful of the growing public adulation, decided to take action. They persuaded one of the disciples, Judas Iscariot, to betray Jesus in return for 30 pieces of silver. One evening, Judas led a group of soldiers to the Garden of Gethsemane, on the slopes of the Mount of Olives. Jesus was walking in the garden when Judas approached him and gave him a kiss – the sign for the soldiers to arrest Jesus.

Crucifixion and Resurrection

Jesus was put on trial by the priests and then passed to Pontius Pilate, the Roman governor of Judea, for sentencing. The priests wanted Pilate to order Jesus' execution, but Pilate could find no reason to put Jesus to death. Instead, he asked the crowd to choose who should be crucified – Jesus or a thief named Barabbas.

By this time, the crowd had turned against Jesus, and decided that *he* should be crucified. Jesus was given a crown of thorns and forced to carry his heavy wooden cross to a hill called Calvary, just outside the city walls. There, he was crucified between two thieves. Calvary is sometimes also known as Golgotha, which means 'the place of the skull'.

The body of Jesus was buried in a tomb cut out of a rock face, and the tomb was sealed with a heavy stone. Three days later, Mary Magdalene discovered that the stone had been rolled to one side and the tomb was empty. She was afraid that

Jesus' body had been stolen, but the Bible tells that Jesus appeared to her and told her he would soon be with his Father in heaven. This 'rising from the dead' is known as the Resurrection.

Spreading the word After Jesus' death, his disciples began to spread his message. They referred to him as Jesus Christ. *Christ* comes from the Greek word *christos*, meaning 'saviour' or 'king'. The disciples preached that Christ had died to save people from their sins and to give them the chance to go to heaven. They told people to abandon their old religion and follow Christ, and to live a virtuous life obeying Christ's teachings. The followers of Christ who spread Christianity are known as the Apostles. Their work is described in the New Testament book, the Acts of the Apostles.

The Acts of the Apostles describes how the Holy Spirit (see panel opposite) appeared to the Apostles and gave them inspiration to carry out their work. About two months after Jesus' death, the Apostles met in Jerusalem to celebrate the Jewish harvest festival known as Pentecost. While they were there, they heard the sound of a powerful

*The Crucifixion has been painted by many leading Christian artists. This painting, **The Crucified Christ with the Virgin Mary, Saints and Angels**, is by the Italian artist Raphael (1483–1520).*

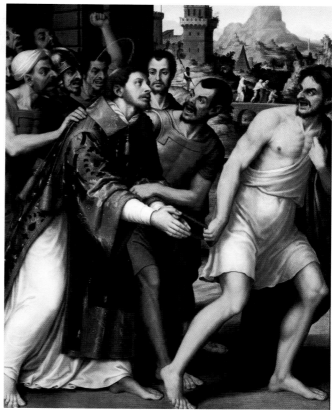

The martyrdom of St Stephen, as seen through the eyes of a 16th-century Spanish artist. Stephen is surrounded by tormenters who are eagerly leading him on to his death.

wind, and saw a flame flickering over each of their heads – a sign that the Holy Spirit was with them. The Apostles found they could speak in many different languages and so went out into the crowds and began to preach. At that time, Jerusalem was full of Jews who had come from many different lands to celebrate Pentecost. The Apostles spoke to them all in their own languages, and told them about Jesus' message.

Gradually, the Christian message spread to all parts of the world where Jewish people lived and small communities of Christians became established all over the Middle East. At first, only Jews converted to Christianity, but slowly Christianity spread to Gentiles (non-Jews) as well.

Martyrs The Apostles made enemies as they spread their new religion. In particular, the Jewish elders were angered that their people were abandoning their faith. Some of the Apostles were put to death for preaching Christianity and opposing the commands of the elders. Stephen was stoned to death outside the walls of Jerusalem, while Peter was thrown into the city prison and later sentenced to death. Stephen and Peter were among the first of many Christian

THE TRINITY

Christians believe that God has three forms: God the Father, God the Son, and God the Holy Spirit. Together, these forms of God are known as the Trinity. God the Son is Jesus Christ. God the Holy Spirit is also known as the Holy Ghost. In Christian art, the Holy Spirit is sometimes shown as a flame or it sometimes takes the form of a white dove.

martyrs. After their deaths, they became saints. *Saint*, from the Latin *sanctus* ('sacred'), is a title conferred on holy people in the Christian religion.

Saint Paul St Paul is one of the most important figures in the early history of Christianity. As a young man he was named Saul, and took part in the Jewish persecution of the Christians. He even joined in the stoning of Stephen. The Acts of the Apostles describes how Saul was converted to Christianity on the road from Jerusalem to Damascus, in northern Palestine. As he approached Damascus, he had a vision of brilliant light, which left him blind for three days. After he had recovered his sight, Saul became a Christian and changed his name to Paul. He spent the rest of his life travelling and spreading the Christian message.

On his first journey, Paul travelled around the lands of the eastern Mediterranean. He reached Cyprus and set up a church in Salamis. Then he returned to the mainland and journeyed around the areas that are now Syria and Turkey. In some places, such as Lystra, Paul was welcomed; in others, he was driven away. On his second journey, Paul set off overland to the cities of Tarsus, Lystra and Antioch (in present-day Turkey). Then he crossed the sea to Philippi (in Macedonia), Athens and Corinth (in Greece), and Ephesus (in Turkey). In all these places, Paul set up new communities of Christians. On his third

Left: *Painting of St Paul from the Church of Saint-Séverin, Paris.*

Below: *The journeys of St Paul. For 25 years, Paul undertook tiring and dangerous journeys over land and sea.*

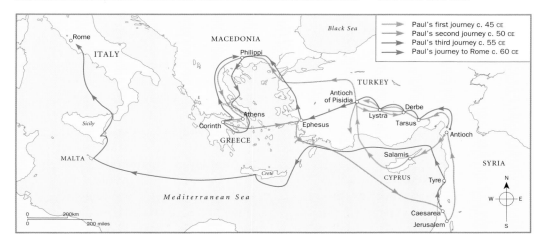

The ancient theatre at Ephesus in Turkey was the scene of a riot against St Paul. Some worshippers of the goddess Diana organized a protest against Paul's teachings, but fortunately the crowd was kept under control.

journey, Paul revisited some of the places he had been to before. While he was in Ephesus, he aroused great anger by trying to prevent people from worshipping the goddess Artemis (known as Diana to the Romans).

On his return to Jerusalem, Paul was arrested and sent to Rome to be tried by the emperor. Paul travelled under guard in a merchant ship, which was wrecked off the coast of Malta. When he finally reached Rome, Paul was placed under house arrest. He spent two years there and during this time, wrote many letters (see panel). Nobody knows how he died, but he may have been beheaded on the orders of Emperor Nero.

The early Church By the end of the first century CE, Christianity was flourishing in many parts of the Roman Empire. The new faith was especially

PAUL'S LETTERS

While he was travelling, Paul wrote letters to the Christian communities he had set up. These letters encouraged the new Christians in their faith and taught them more about their religion. Later, Paul's letters were included in the New Testament. Perhaps the most famous of all Paul's letters are his *Letters to the Corinthians.* They include a well-known passage about love. In this passage, Paul explains that Christians should love each other and all other people: *Above all remember that without love you are nothing.*

popular in Rome, but many powerful Romans were suspicious of Christianity, so most early Christians did not reveal their faith. Instead, they met secretly in believers' houses, usually on a Sunday, early in the morning or in the evening. The Christians prayed together, sang hymns and studied the scriptures. They also celebrated Holy Communion as a reminder of Christ's Last Supper (see page 42) and his death and resurrection.

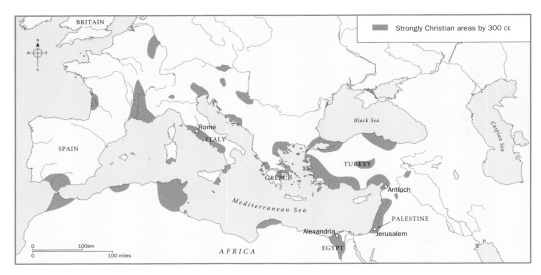

This map shows the Christian areas around the Mediterranean Sea at the end of the third century CE. Christianity had also reached parts of northern Europe along the routes of major rivers.

Persecution Some Roman emperors saw the growing popularity of Christianity as a serious threat, and took harsh measures to try and wipe out the new religion. In 64 CE, Emperor Nero blamed the Christians for the Great Fire of Rome. He organized their persecution in dreadful ways. Christians were wrapped in animal skins and thrown to the dogs, or used as human torches to light up the emperor's parties. Nero also turned the killing of Christians into public entertainment.

CHRISTIAN SIGNS

The early Christians used secret signs to show that they shared the same faith. These symbols included a fish, an anchor and a dove. The symbol that Constantine chose to paint on his soldiers' shields was the chi-rho sign. It is made up of the first two letters of the word *Christ* in Greek.

They were sent into the arenas of public amphitheatres to be attacked and eaten by lions. Other Roman emperors had Christians arrested, tortured and killed, but Emperor Diocletian carried out the most savage persecution. In 303 CE, he began executing thousands of Christians for refusing to give up their faith. He also ordered the burning of all Christian texts and the destruction of their homes.

Bishops, deacons and priests

In spite of the persecutions, Christianity continued to grow. By the start of the second century CE, the Christian communities had begun to organize themselves. Groups of Christians built churches where they met regularly for simple services. Each major city had its own bishop, responsible for all the Christians in the surrounding area. The bishops were helped by deacons and priests. The deacons took care of practical matters, such as giving help to the poor, while the priests travelled from church to church, leading services. To keep the

Christian Church united, the bishops communicated with each other as much as possible. By the third century, the leading bishops were based in Rome, Alexandria (Egypt) and Antioch (Turkey).

Constantine and the Christians

Emperor Diocletian died in 305 CE, and the following year a new and ambitious ruler called Constantine came to power. At this stage in its history, the Roman Empire was divided in two: Constantine shared control of the Western Empire with Maxentius, while two other rulers controlled the Eastern Empire.

In 312 CE, Constantine fought Maxentius at the Battle of Milvian Bridge, close to Rome. Just before the battle, he had a vision, seeing a cross of light in the sky and hearing a voice saying 'Conquer by this sign'. Constantine immediately gave orders for all his soldiers to paint the Christian Chi-rho symbol on their shields (see panel on page 49). His army was victorious, and Constantine became convinced that he should support the Christians in his empire.

After his victory over Maxentius, Constantine announced that Christians throughout the Western Empire were free to follow their religion. This famous announcement, made in 313 CE, was known as the Edict of Milan. Constantine also gave money to the bishops to build large churches, or basilicas, including the magnificent St Peter's Basilica in Rome. He declared that Sunday should be a day of rest, and paid for new copies of the scriptures to be made.

UNDERGROUND MEETINGS

In the city of Rome, Christians often held secret meetings in the catacombs, a series of caverns and tunnels under the city that were used as burial places. Christian paintings and altars dating from the fourth century have been found in these ancient tunnels.

The remains of the Catacomb of Priscilla, beneath the city of Rome. Some of the catacombs where early Christians met had paintings of Jesus on their walls.

ISOLATED LIVES

Some Christians chose to spend their lives as hermits, living alone in isolated regions. One famous hermit, St Simon Stylites, spent 30 years sitting on top of a pillar! But not everyone wanted to live as a hermit. In the fourth century, single-sex communities comprised of monks or nuns began to form, people who dedicated their lives to prayer and contemplaton, isolated from the rest of society.

This Roman coin shows the Emperor Constantine wearing a crown of olive leaves. It was made in France around 306 CE.

In 324 CE, Emperor Constantine defeated the rulers of the Eastern Empire and took control of the whole Roman Empire. Three years later, he moved his capital from Rome to the city of Byzantium (present-day Istanbul), which he renamed Constantinople. Constantine established Constantinople as a Christian city and endowed it with many fine churches.

The Council of Nicaea

During Constantine's rule, a violent argument broke out between two Christian thinkers. Arius, an Egyptian priest, claimed that Christ was created by God, whereas Athanasius, bishop of Alexandria, said that Christ was part of God and had existed from the beginning of time. With the argument threatening to split the Church,

Constantine took action. In 325 CE he summoned all the bishops to a meeting at the Council of Nicaea (in present-day Turkey) to support Athanasius. They wrote a statement of their beliefs, later known as the Nicene Creed. The Creed is still recited by Christians today. It states that God the Son is 'of one substance with the Father'.

A state religion About 25 years after Constantine's death, the emperor Julian tried to bring back the Roman gods and goddesses, but it was too late to stop the growth of Christianity. All the emperors after Julian supported the Christians, and in 391 CE Emperor Theodosius declared Christianity the empire's official religion. By this time, the Christian Church had become wealthy and powerful. Christians built grand churches and held elaborate services, with chanting and singing.

During the fourth century CE, the bishops held several councils to establish the format of services and to fix the times of the great festivals of the Christian calendar. The bishop of Rome played a leading role at these councils and gradually assumed the role of head of the Church, gaining the new title of pope.

The fall of the Roman Empire

By the 350s, the Roman Empire was under threat from barbarian tribes, most of them pagans who worshipped their own gods. In 401 CE, an army of Visigoths attacked the city of Milan in northern Italy, and in 410 CE they invaded Rome. The Romans fought back, but could not stop hordes of Vandals and other tribes from pouring into Germany and France. In 409 CE, the Vandals invaded Spain; 20 years later they conquered North Africa. From here, the Vandals moved into Italy, and in 455 CE they spent 12 days looting Rome. The Roman Empire in the west finally collapsed in 476 CE. This was a major blow for Christianity.

ST AUGUSTINE OF HIPPO

St Augustine was bishop of Hippo in North Africa from 396 to 430 CE. He was a theologian and philosopher who wrote many books on the Christian faith. In particular, Augustine believed that sinners may be forgiven through God's grace. Augustine strongly influenced the development of Christian teaching and is known as one of the Fathers of the Church. Having witnessed the collapse of the Roman Empire, he wrote a famous book, *The City of God*, in which he stressed the importance of a united Christian community, separate from the state.

A detail from an Italian painting of St Augustine.

The early Middle Ages After the fall of Rome, the Western Empire split into small barbarian kingdoms. In many parts of Europe Christianity died out completely, but the Church survived in Rome. Some monasteries also survived, and monks kept Christian learning alive by copying out holy texts. The Church entered a long period of missionary activity and expansion across the world. One of the first areas to be converted to Christianity was Ireland. In the first half of the fifth century CE, St Patrick set up Christian monasteries in many parts of Ireland. These monasteries provided a base for other missionaries, who took the Christian message to Britain and France.

In 596 CE, Pope Gregory the Great sent a monk named Augustine to preach to the Angles in southern England. Two centuries later, the English monk St Boniface converted the tribes of

A stone carving of St Patrick at the entrance to the Chapel Royal in Dublin, Ireland.

present-day Germany. The Viking people of Scandinavia took longer to accept the faith, but by the 11th century there were churches in Denmark, Sweden and Norway.

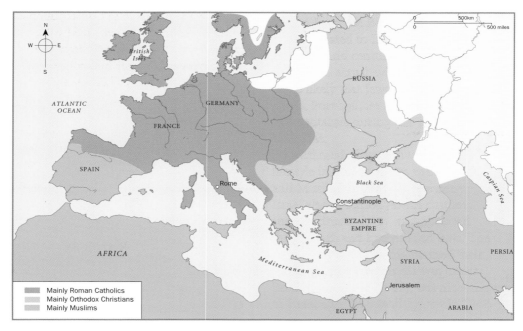

The Churches of the East and West after the split in 1054. The map also shows the extent of Islam (the Muslim religion) at this time.

While the Church in the West was slowly rebuilding itself, the Church in the eastern part of the Roman Empire was thriving. The capital of the Eastern Roman (Byzantine) Empire was Constantinople, which became a key centre of Christianity. From here, missionaries took the message eastwards. In the ninth century, St Cyril and St Methodius took the Christian message to the Slavs in eastern Europe, and in 988 Prince Vladimir of Russia declared that all Russians should be baptized as Christians.

Christianity also spread through Syria and Persia, but many Christians in these areas rebelled against the standard teachings of the Church. In Syria the rebels were known as Monophysites, and in Persia they were called Nestorians. Neither of these groups was recognized by the leaders of the Church.

In the seventh century, the new religion of Islam began in Arabia. Within a hundred years, Islam had established itself in large areas of the Middle East, North Africa and southern Spain. A few Christian communities survived in these areas, but they were greatly outnumbered by Muslims.

CHRISTIANITY IN ETHIOPIA

In the fourth century CE, a Christian missionary named Frumentius was shipwrecked off the coast of Ethiopia, in North Africa. He converted the king of the ancient Ethiopian kingdom of Axum. Two centuries later, the area that is now Sudan also became Christian. Even after North Africa was taken over by Muslim rulers, Ethiopia remained a largely Christian kingdom.

theological and doctrinal matters, such as the source of the Holy Spirit (did the Spirit proceed from the Father, or from the Father *and* the Son?) and whether leavened or unleavened bread should be used in Holy Communion. After much debate, in 1054 there was a split. The Eastern Church was led by the patriarch in Constantinople, and the Western Church was led by the pope in Rome. The Eastern Church later became known as the Orthodox Church, and the Western Church became the Roman Catholic Church.

The East–West split

Gradually, the Church in the East became increasingly independent from that in the West. They disagreed on several

The city of Constantinople (which later became Istanbul) was the heart of the Eastern Church and was full of splendid church buildings. This photograph shows the dome of the Church of Hagia Sophia in Istanbul.

The growth of the monasteries

During the fourth and fifth centuries CE, the monasteries became more organized, due in part to the actions of two men: St Basil (see panel) and St Benedict.

St Benedict of Nursia, the father of Western monasticsm, was born in northern Italy in 480. He began his religious life as a hermit, but soon decided it was preferable for monks to live together in a community. He established a famous monastery at Monte Cassino and wrote a set of guidelines for his monks to follow. According to St Benedict's rule, monks should divide their time between prayer, study and hard physical work, such as farming. He taught his followers to meet together to worship at regular times of day. He also taught that monks should eat plain food, wear simple clothes (called habits) and look after the sick and the poor. After Benedict's death, Benedictine monasteries were established all over western Europe.

ORTHODOX MONASTERIES

In the mid-fourth century, St Basil the Great founded a monastery in Pontus (south of the Black Sea). He wrote a set of rules for his monks, instructing them to pray, carry out good works, to help the sick and the poor, and to study the Bible. Over the next few centuries, many more monasteries were founded in Turkey and Greece, all of them following St Basil's rules.

A medieval painting showing St Benedict giving his blessing to the members of his order.

This map shows some of the most important Christian monasteries in the Middle Ages, as well as the places where religious orders were founded.

In the tenth century, Abbot Odilo became the new head of the Benedictine monastery of Cluny in central France. He established a new kind of monastic community that concentrated on learning, music and art. Cluniac monasteries soon spread all over France. Their buildings were beautifully decorated, and the Cluniac monks held elaborate services. However, another French abbot, St Bernard of Clairvaux, reacted against the richness of the Cluniac monasteries. He set up the Cistercians, a new order of monks who led a simple life of prayer in much plainer buildings. The Cistercian movement became very popular in the 12th and 13th centuries.

Franciscans and Dominicans

In the early 13th century, friars were members of certain mendicant religious orders. Like monks, they lived simple lives, but spent most of their time travelling around, preaching and caring for the poor and sick. Two men were responsible for the growth of the friars: St Dominic and St Francis. St Dominic was a Spanish missionary who had devoted himself to trying to convert heretics. In 1215, he founded an order of preachers specializing in teaching, who later became known as the Dominicans. The first Dominican community was based near Carcassonne in southern France.

St Francis came from the Italian town of Assisi. He led a holy life, teaching and caring for the poor and soon attracted many followers. In 1209, he established the order of Franciscan friars in Assisi. Three years later, St Clare, a friend of St Francis, set up the Order of the Poor Clares for women. Like the Franciscans, the Poor Clares lived in simple buildings and spent most of their time in prayer and helping the poor.

Holy Roman Empire

During the Middle Ages, the popes frequently received support from western Europe's powerful secular rulers, but the Church and the rulers also often clashed. One of the Church's great early supporters was the emperor Charlemagne. He became leader of the Franks in 768 and built up a large Christian empire covering most of present-day Germany and France. In 800, Pope Leo III crowned Charlemagne emperor of the Romans (Holy Roman Emperor), and Charlemagne promised to support the Church in return. This alliance with Charlemagne gave the Church a great deal of power. However, after his death, Charlemagne's empire collapsed.

In 955, the German king Otto I won control of large parts of central and eastern Europe. The pope granted him the title of Holy Roman Emperor, which gave Otto and his descendents control over all the bishops and their lands. The emperors used the bishops to help them rule, but the popes wanted to control the bishops themselves, also hoping to gain money from the bishops' lands. Between the 11th and 13th centuries, the popes and emperors fought bitterly over their rights to control the bishops.

A map of medieval Europe, showing the followers of the rival popes, based in Avignon and Rome. The Holy Roman emperors kept changing sides, sometimes supporting one pope, sometimes the other.

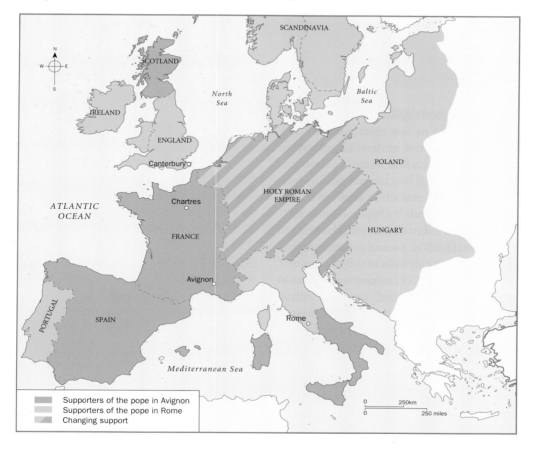

Supporters of the pope in Avignon
Supporters of the pope in Rome
Changing support

Rival popes In 1309, two men competed for the title of pope. One of them appealed to the French king for help and moved the seat of the papacy to Avignon in southern France, while his rival stayed in Rome. For the next hundred years, while the official popes were based in France, for part of this time rival popes also ruled in Rome. Some western European countries followed the Avignon pope, while others supported the pope in Rome. The situation was made more complicated by the Holy Roman emperors, who kept changing sides. It led to a major split called the Great Western Schism, which greatly weakened the power of the Roman Catholic popes and bishops.

Crusades By the end of the 11th century, many Christians had become concerned about the Holy Land. For some 400 years, Palestine had been ruled by Muslim Turks, and for the most part they had allowed Christian pilgrims to travel to Jerusalem. However, by the 1090s, relations between the Turks and Christians had deteriorated, and some pilgrims had been attacked. Christians in the Eastern Church felt especially threatened. The Turkish lands lay adjacent to the Christian Byzantine Empire, and the Turks were

gradually gaining Byzantine lands. This alarmed Christians in both east and west. In 1095, Pope Urban II gave a sermon urging all Christians to go on a 'holy war', or Crusade, to drive the Muslims out of the Holy Land. Nobles from France, Germany and Italy gathered their armies and embarked for the Middle East, on what was the start of the First Crusade.

PILGRIMAGES

Medieval Christians would often go on pilgrimages. They travelled long distances to holy shrines, where saints were buried or sacred objects kept. Pilgrims made these journeys in the hope that God would forgive them their sins and cure their diseases. Popular destinations for pilgrimage included Jerusalem and Rome. In England, pilgrims visited the shrine of St Thomas Becket in Canterbury. Becket was an archbishop who quarrelled with King Henry II and was murdered in 1170 by the king's knights.

This painting comes from an illustrated version of the Canterbury Tales *by Geoffrey Chaucer. The* Canterbury Tales, *written in the 14th century, introduces a group of pilgrims travelling from London to Canterbury and telling stories along the way.*

In 1099, the Crusaders captured Jerusalem and the surrounding lands. Some of them stayed on to defend their newly conquered territory, but many Crusaders returned home. In 1144, a Muslim army seized the city of Edessa (in present-day Turkey), but the Second Crusade failed to win it back. In 1187, the Muslims, led by Saladin, recaptured Jerusalem.

The Third Crusade was led by the rulers of France, England and Germany. They won many battles and captured the city of Acre, but again failed to win back Jerusalem. The Fourth Crusade only reached as far as Constantinople. Here, the Crusaders turned on the Byzantines and took over their city. Crusaders from western Europe ruled Constantinople for the next 60 years and sent many Byzantine treasures back home. This period was to engender deep bitterness between the Eastern and Western churches.

Over the next 100 years there were three more Crusades, but the Christians did not win any major new lands. In 1229, the Muslims allowed the Christians to take over Jerusalem. However, the agreement did not last. In 1244, a Muslim army recaptured Jerusalem, and in 1291 the Muslims finally conquered Acre, the last Crusader city. This marked the end of the Crusades.

CRUSADER KNIGHTS

During the Crusades, new orders of warrior monks were formed, known as Crusader knights. These men lived like monks, dedicating their lives to God, but they were also fierce warriors. The main orders of Crusader knights were the Knights Templar, the Knights Hospitaller and the Teutonic Knights.

A medieval artist's impression of the capture of the city of Antioch. The Crusaders won Antioch from the Muslim Turks during the First Crusade.

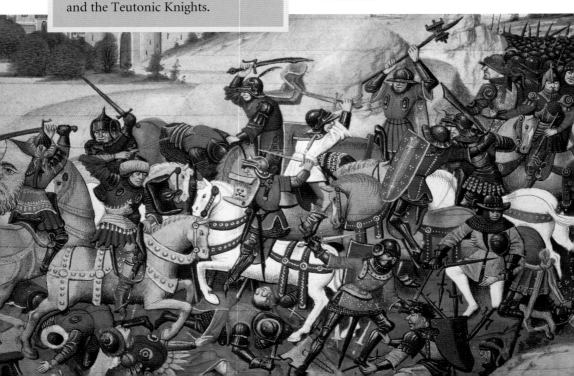

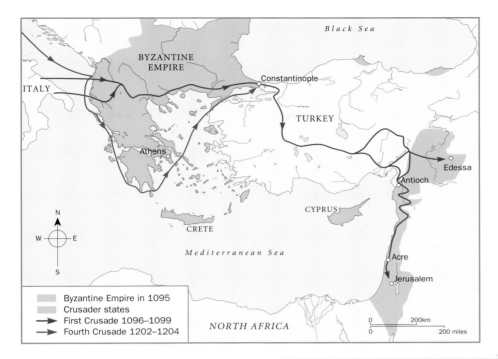

This map shows the routes taken by different Crusades and the land won by the Crusaders.

Martin Luther

By the early 1500s, many people in western Europe were unhappy with the Roman Catholic Church. Too many Church leaders seemed interested only in wealth and power, and people complained that their parish priests were badly educated and lazy. In particular, the Church was blamed for the sale of indulgences (pardons for people's sins). The rich paid large sums for these indulgences, while the poor could not afford to have their sins absolved.

In 1517, a German priest called Martin Luther compiled his Ninety-Five Theses, a list of ways in which the Catholic Church ought to be reformed. He nailed this list to the church door in Wittenberg, northern Germany, and his ideas soon spread. Church leaders were furious, and in 1520 the pope excommunicated Luther. The priest went into hiding but continued working on his ideas for a reform of the

A PLAINER PROTESTANT STYLE

Protestant churches are generally much plainer in style than Roman Catholic churches. Unlike Catholic churches, there are no statues of the Virgin Mary or the saints, since Protestants believe that they should communicate directly with God and Jesus rather than pray to Mary and the saints. The one exception to this practice is the Anglican Church, which took over the buildings of the Roman Catholics and retained some of the characteristics of that faith.

Church. He believed that church services should be kept simple and that people should read the Bible for themselves rather than have it read to them by a priest. Luther helped make this possible by translating the New Testament from Greek into German.

Luther had intended to reform the Catholic Church from the inside, but by the 1520s it was clear that this was impossible. Gradually, people all over Germany began to hold simple services based on Luther's ideas, and the Lutheran Church was born. By the 1550s, Lutheranism had spread to Denmark, Norway and Sweden. Other Protestant churches followed the example of the Lutherans and held simple services with readings from the Bible and the singing of hymns.

The printing press
The development of printing played a key role in the rapid spread of Luther's ideas. In 1436, Johannes Gutenberg from Mainz, Germany, invented the movable-type printing press and by 1500 there were presses all over Europe, but especially in Germany. Luther was a gifted and popular writer who wrote many pamphlets, which were read widely. Thanks to the printing press, ordinary people could also read Luther's translation of the Bible.

Calvinism
John Calvin was a French priest who broke away from the Roman Catholic Church. In 1541, he established a group of Protestants in Geneva, Switzerland. Like Luther, Calvin emphasized the importance of the Bible in Christian worship. He also claimed that some chosen people would be saved and go to heaven, while others would go to hell. Calvin wrote several books on the Bible that were read by many in Europe. Calvinism was very popular in Switzerland, and it also spread to Scotland and the Netherlands.

Henry VIII's rebellion
The English Protestant Reformation began when King Henry VIII quarrelled with

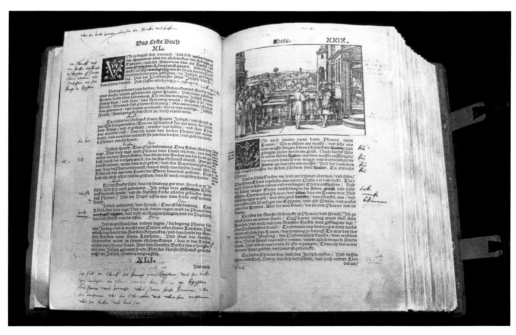

One of the earliest copies of Luther's Bible, translated from Greek into German. This copy was owned by Luther himself and includes notes and corrections made by him.

The dissolution of the monasteries, by King Henry VIII, led to many fine buildings falling into ruins. One of the many ruined monasteries is Rievaulx Abbey in Yorkshire, England.

the pope. Henry wanted to divorce his first wife, Catherine of Aragon, and marry his mistress, Anne Boleyn, but the pope refused to grant him a divorce. This made Henry so angry that he decided to break away from the Catholic Church. In an act of Parliament of 1534, Henry was named supreme head of the Church of England, marking the start of the Anglican Church.

In some ways the Anglican Church simply continued the practices of the Roman Catholic Church. It still had bishops and parish priests, and it took over all the Catholic cathedrals and churches. However, there were some important differences. Bibles were placed in Anglican churches for the public to read, and services were held in English, not Latin. In 1549, the Archbishop of

THE PRESBYTERIAN CHURCH

The Presbyterian Church began in Scotland in the 1560s. It was founded by John Knox, who had spent several years as a preacher at a Calvinist church in Geneva, Switzerland. In the Presbyterian Church there is no fixed form of worship, and each congregation is governed by a group of presbyters, or elders, who are all of equal rank. When James I became king of England in 1603, he recognized Presbyterianism as the national faith in Scotland. Presbyterianism later spread to England, Wales, Ireland and North America.

Canterbury, Thomas Cranmer, produced *The Book of Common Prayer*, which set out all the rites and services of the Anglican Church. Today, Anglicans around the world still use prayer books based on Cranmer's original work.

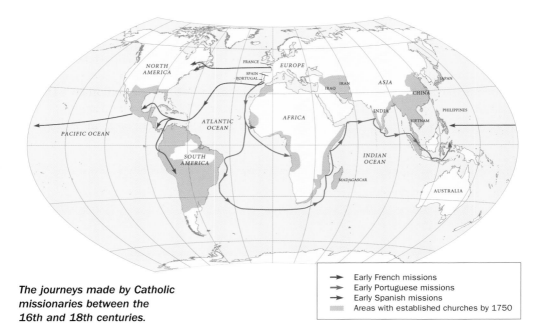

The journeys made by Catholic missionaries between the 16th and 18th centuries.

→ Early French missions
→ Early Portuguese missions
→ Early Spanish missions
▨ Areas with established churches by 1750

In 1538, Henry VIII began a campaign to dissolve the Catholic monasteries in England. It was well known that many monks and nuns did not lead holy lives, but Henry also wanted to destroy the power and wealth of the Catholic Church in his kingdom, and at the same time swell the royal coffers by selling off Church lands. Some of the monastery buildings were sold to wealthy nobles, but many others simply fell into ruins.

The Counter-Reformation

As the Reformation gathered strength, Roman Catholic leaders tried hard to win people back to their Church. They began a reform movement of their own, which became known as the Counter-Reformation. Some of the first areas of reform concerned the monasteries. The existing monastic orders were reformed and several new orders were created. Catholic leaders set up training colleges for priests, built elaborate new cathedrals and churches, and attacked the Protestants

in sermons and books. From 1545 to 1563, the leaders of the Church met together in a group known as the Council of Trent. They used the ecumenical council to restate their beliefs, condemn Protestant ideas and plan reforms to the Church.

The most famous of the new monastic orders was the Society of Jesus, also known as the Jesuits. The Jesuits were founded in 1534 by the Spanish monk Ignatius of Loyola. They lived a life of extreme discipline and devotion to Christ, and promised to carry out any task the pope demanded of them. The Jesuits ran schools and colleges and travelled as missionaries, first to Poland and then to more distant lands.

From the early 1500s onwards, Catholic missionaries began accompanying conquering armies to newly discovered lands in South America, Africa and Asia. Jesuit missionaries were especially adventurous. Francis Xavier, for example, led missions to India, Sri Lanka and Japan in the 1540s and 1550s, while in 1582 Matteo Ricci travelled to China, where he remained for the next 20 years. By the start of the 17th century, Catholic missionaries had converted hundreds of thousands to Christianity and had set up churches, monasteries and schools in many parts of Asia and South America. However, not all the missions were successful. In the 1640s, a group of French Jesuit missionaries in Canada were put to death by Native Americans.

Religious wars In many parts of Europe, the clash between Protestants and Catholics led to war. In Germany, Lutherans and Catholics fought each other in the Thirty Years' War (1618–1648), while in France, French Protestants, or Huguenots, fought the Catholic king and his supporters. The most horrific event during the wars fought in France was the St Bartholomew's Day Massacre of 1572 when thousands of Huguenots were killed on a single day.

BAROQUE ART

During the period of the Counter-Reformation, a new, very elaborate style of religious art and architecture developed, called Baroque. It was popular with many Roman Catholic leaders because it played on people's emotions and encouraged them to be more devout. Baroque painters and sculptors, such as Gian Lorenzo Bernini, produced dramatic images of saints experiencing miraculous visions, and martyrs suffering terrible deaths.

The Ecstasy of Saint Teresa was created by Gian Lorenzo Bernini between 1647 and 1652. Works like this had a powerful emotional effect on Catholic Christians.

Puritans During the 16th century, some English Protestants became unhappy with the Anglican Church under Queen Elizabeth I (1558–1603). The Puritans disapproved of all finery and show. They dressed very plainly and followed a simple form of worship. By the 1650s, the Puritans had gained political power in England. In the previous decade there had been a power struggle between the English king, Charles I, and parliament, leading to a civil war (1642–1649). Parliament's forces were triumphant, and one of their leaders, Oliver Cromwell, took power. Cromwell was a Puritan and, from 1653 to 1658, he ruled England according to Puritan principles. He closed down many ale houses and discouraged dancing and theatre-going. However, in 1660, Charles I's son, Charles II, became king and made Anglicanism the official religion of England.

Baptists Like the Puritans, the Baptists were a breakaway group from the Anglican Church. Originally known as Separatists, they were persecuted in England and escaped to Holland in 1608. The Separatists returned to England in 1612 and attracted many followers. By the 18th century, the Baptist Church was well established in Europe and America. Baptists only baptize adult believers – by total immersion in water – because Christ was not baptized until he was an adult.

Christians in North America

In 1620, the Pilgrims – a group of Puritans and Separatists – set sail from England bound for North America. They arrived in Plymouth, Massachusetts, on the east coast and established a colony there. Over the next century, Protestants from England, Scotland, Germany and the Netherlands all made the journey to North America. Most of them settled in the east and north of the continent, and these areas became strongly Protestant.

In the 1500s, the Spanish had settled the western part of North America, while the French had owned large areas of land in the centre of the continent, until they sold it to the United States in the 19th century. Hence in both the central and western areas of North America, Roman

Once the Pilgrims had become settled in Plymouth, they held a service of thanksgiving to God. This painting shows the first sermon delivered in Plymouth.

QUAKERS

The Society of Friends – or the Quakers – was founded in England around 1650. Quakers gather in meeting houses rather than churches and they stress the importance of quiet meditation. Soon after the Society of Friends was formed, some Quakers travelled to North America, but they faced persecution from the larger Christian groups already there. In the 1670s, a Quaker named William Penn began buying up land for the Quakers in the area that would later become Pennsylvania. Today, a number of Quaker organizations have their headquarters in Pennsylvania.

Catholicism was the main religion of the European settlers.

In the 1730s, a young church minister called Jonathan Edwards began to travel around the east coast of the USA preaching with great passion. Edwards' sermons had a dramatic effect on his listeners and won thousands of converts to Christianity. Edwards' followers built new churches all over New England, and he inspired many other preachers to spread the word. This dramatic movement later became known as the First Great Awakening.

The North American colonies in 1750, showing the main Christian groups. The Lutheran and Congregationalist Churches both had a strong following, but no single religious group dominated the colonies.

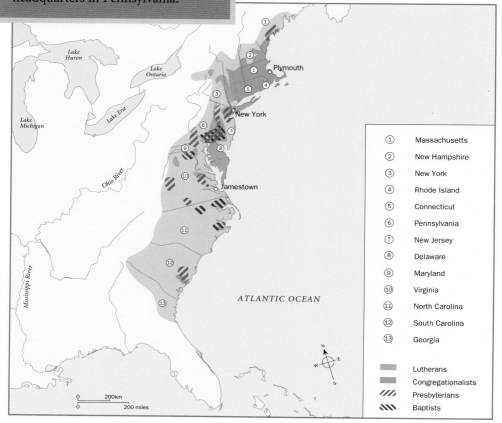

①	Massachusetts
②	New Hampshire
③	New York
④	Rhode Island
⑤	Connecticut
⑥	Pennsylvania
⑦	New Jersey
⑧	Delaware
⑨	Maryland
⑩	Virginia
⑪	North Carolina
⑫	South Carolina
⑬	Georgia

Lutherans
Congregationalists
Presbyterians
Baptists

John Wesley and the Methodists

In the 18th century, some Christian preachers began to travel from place to place, spreading their message of salvation. They held open-air meetings in which they preached and encouraged people to pray and sing hymns together. This type of worship, in which the Christian message is taken into the wider world, is often known as evangelism. One of the first evangelist Christians was John Wesley, who developed Methodism.

Wesley trained as an Anglican minister, but in 1738 he experienced what became known as his evangelical conversion. He began to spread the message that Christians could be saved from their sins. At first, he preached his message in Anglican churches, but later he travelled around the country holding open-air meetings wherever he went.

Methodists hold simple services, which involve the singing of rousing hymns and the preaching of passionate sermons. They also aim to live a virtuous life and help the poor. John Wesley ensured that the Methodist Church was well organized, and used travelling preachers to spread the word. His movement grew rapidly in Britain and the USA.

New revival and revelations

Around the end of the 18th century, a powerful new wave of religious feeling swept through the USA. Known as the Second Great Awakening, it started with 'camp meetings' held in tents in Kentucky and Tennessee. People stayed for days in the camps, listening to fiery sermons and being baptized in their thousands in the local rivers. Later, this Christian revival spread to the East Coast, where powerful preachers such as Lyman Beecher and Charles Finney drew enormous crowds. Many of the newly converted Christians worked to change American society. In particular, the Second Great Awakening led many to campaign against slavery.

During the 19th century, several new Christian sects were founded in the USA, usually by someone who preached a new 'revelation' of the Bible's message.

Africa in 1914, showing all the areas reached by Christian missionaries. The map also shows the ancient Christian community of Ethiopia.

Mediterranean Sea

Sahara Desert

Nile

Senegal

Niger

Lake Chad

White Nile

Blue Nile

Lake Victoria

INDIAN OCEAN

Congo

ATLANTIC OCEAN

Zambezi

Kalahari Desert

0   1000km
0   1000 miles

Missionary activity by 1914
Ethiopian Church (founded 4th century)
Mainly Muslim area

THE SALVATION ARMY

In 1861, Methodist minister William Booth and his wife Catherine began a Christian mission to help the poor in the East End of London. To carry out this work, Booth set up an organization called the Salvation Army. Its members dressed in easily recognizable uniforms and held lively services in the street, attracting large crowds with their cheerful band music. As well as preaching the Gospel, the Salvation Army offered food and shelter to people in need. By 1912, it had branches in more than 50 countries.

Some of the most successful sects were the Mormons, the Christian Scientists and the Jehovah's Witnesses. These three religious groups soon gained large numbers of followers around the world.

Christian missionaries

By the 1850s, countries such as Britain, Germany and France had acquired extensive overseas colonies in Africa and Asia. Christians were determined to spread their faith to these areas, and missionaries from Europe travelled to all parts of their country's empires and beyond. By 1900, Christian missionaries had managed to establish churches in almost every country in the world. Many did more than build churches and teach Christianity. They also set up hospitals and schools and helped introduce new farming methods. A major part of missionary work involved providing people with copies of the Bible in their own language, so they could read it for themselves. By 1900, the New Testament had been translated into over 500 languages.

Evangeline Booth, daughter of William and Catherine Booth, was for many years one of the leaders of the Salvation Army. Here she is shown raising money for the Salvation Army's work.

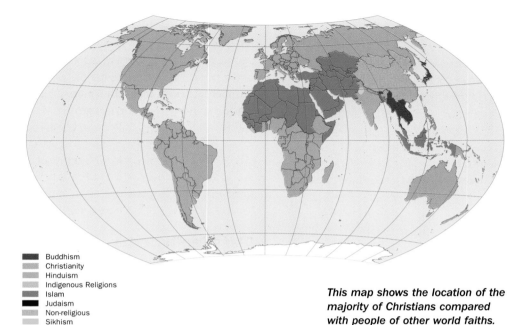

Buddhism	
Christianity	
Hinduism	
Indigenous Religions	
Islam	
Judaism	
Non-religious	
Sikhism	

This map shows the location of the majority of Christians compared with people of other world faiths.

The Charismatic movement

Around the start of the 20th century, a new Christian movement called the Pentecostal Church, began in Los Angeles, California. Pentecostal Christians are now often known as Charismatic Christians, or simply Charismatics. They hold very lively services in which everyone takes part in a wholehearted way, and some of their members claim to have the gifts of prophecy and healing. By the 1950s, the Charismatic movement had spread throughout the world. In 2011, the movement had an estimated 305 million members[1], making it the fastest-growing movement within the Christian Church worldwide. Today, it is especially popular in South America.

Modern evangelism
In the 1950s, there was a new surge in evangelism, as people spread the Christian message

through exciting sermons and rousing hymns. Evangelism was especially popular in the USA, where it was helped greatly by the emergence of television as a mass medium. The leading evangelist of the 20th century was the American preacher Billy Graham. He has travelled around the world many times, speaking to an estimated 210 million people in 185 countries.

Over the last 20 years, a growing number of 'televangelists' have spread their message through television. As well as conducting televised services, some also provide commentary on current events. In the USA, several TV channels are devoted entirely to programmes with a strong Christian message.

Liberation theology
In the 1970s, a new movement began within the Roman Catholic Church in South America. Known as liberation theology, it is based on the idea that Christians have a duty to help the poor and the suffering. Followers of liberation theology believe that they should

[1] http://www.pewforum.org/2011/12/19/global-christianity-exec/

THE ORTHODOX CHURCH

Following its split from the Roman Catholic Church in 1054, the Orthodox Church followed a quite different path. In 1453, Constantinople was conquered by Muslim Turks and the Orthodox Church struggled to survive in Turkey and the Middle East. It continued to thrive in Greece and Russia, however, with each country developing its own traditions.

In 1922, Russia formed the Soviet Union, a Communist and atheist state. The Soviet leaders saw Christianity as a major threat, and within a few years more than a thousand bishops and priests had been executed, and hundreds of monasteries had been destroyed. Persecution of Christians continued until the collapse of the Soviet Union in 1991. Since then, the Russian Orthodox Church has experienced a dramatic revival.

defend their country's people against systems of government that keep some people rich and powerful at the expense of the poor, who form the majority. A number of priests in South America have made a stand against corrupt governments, and several have been killed. Archbishop Oscar Romero of El Salvador was murdered in 1980 for standing up for the rights of the poor in his country. Pope Francis, who took office in 2013, has expressed support for some of the ideas of liberation theology.

Christianity today Christianity is the world's largest religion today. Over a third of the world's population describe themselves as Christians. With more than two billion Christians worldwide, Christianity has almost twice as many followers as Islam, the world's second largest faith.

The American evangelist Billy Graham has converted millions of people to Christianity. He is shown here preaching in New York.

Christianity is thriving in many parts of Asia. In 2004, around 100,000 South Koreans held a prayer meeting in a football stadium to celebrate Easter.

Fundamentalists

The Christian fundamentalist movement began in the USA in the early 20th century as a reaction to the growing lack of faith in modern society. Since then it has grown dramatically, although most of its followers remain in the USA. Fundamentalist Christians wish to return to the basics (or fundamentals) of their religion, and believe in the literal truth of the Bible as the word of God. They campaign for strict moral standards in public and private life.

In Africa, much of Asia and parts of South America, Christianity is growing very fast. But in Europe and, to a lesser extent, the USA, the Christian religion is in decline. Attendance at church services in Europe has fallen dramatically since the 1960s. To take one example, in 2014, just 4.5 per cent of people in France attended church on a weekly basis.[2] In the USA, historically a very devout country, less than 20 per cent go to church every week, and thousands of churches close down each year.[3]

Many fundamentalists believe that God created the world in seven days. These 'creationists' reject the theory of evolution which states that humans and apes share a common ancestor.

Women priests By the end of the 20th century, several Christian groups had decided to ordain women as priests or ministers. The Danish Lutherans led the way when they elected their first female priest in 1947. American Methodists and Presbyterians began ordaining women in 1956, and in 1988 the American Episcopal Church (the American branch of the Anglican Church) elected its first woman bishop.

[2] http://pulitzercenter.org/reporting/europe-italy-catholic-church-millennial-problem-faith

[3] http://www.huffingtonpost.com/steve-mcswain/why-nobody-wants-to-go-to_b_4086016.html

In 1994, the Anglicans approved the ordination of women priests. However, there is still resistance to the idea in the Roman Catholic and Orthodox churches.

Coming together In recent years, the different denominations (or branches) of the Christian Church have made considerable efforts to understand each other and even work together. These efforts to encourage cooperation are known as the ecumenical movement. In 1948, the World Council of Churches was founded to encourage the ecumenical spirit. On a smaller scale, there are many shared activities between different denominations in local communities.

In 1964, Pope Paul VI met Patriarch Athenagoras in Jerusalem. This was the first major attempt to heal the division between the Roman Catholic and Orthodox churches since their split in 1054. Since this visit, there have been more meetings the heads of the two churches.

One outstanding example of the ecumenical spirit is the Taizé community, founded by a Swiss monk, Brother Roger, in the French town of Taizé near Lyons. The Taizé brothers hold simple services that can be shared by people of all denominations. Every year, thousands of people flock to Taizé to worship together.

Sisters of the Missionaries of Charity of Mother Teresa at mass in the chapel of the Mother House, Kolkata, India.

GIVING AID

Some Christians see it as their duty to help those suffering from poverty, hunger and disease. Christian charities, such as Christian Aid, send money and support to people who are suffering, and numerous brave individuals devote their lives to helping others. In many parts of the world, Christians have set up hospitals and caring communities, which are often run by monks and nuns. The most famous of these is Mother Teresa, who devoted her life to helping the poor and homeless in India.

CHAPTER 3
ISLAM

ISLAM was born in the harsh desert environment of sixth-century Arabia. Many of the Arabs, the inhabitants of the Arabian Peninsula, followed a nomadic existence, moving from place to place with their herds. Others cultivated the land with the little water that was available, while a minority lived in towns. All people looked to their clan, or tribe, for protection. The region was influenced by several religious traditions. The Byzantine Empire was the most important Christian empire in the region, and Christianity held sway in southern Arabia. In the Sasanian Empire, based in Persia (Iran), a religion called Zoroastrianism was practised. Throughout the region there were small Jewish communities. Most Arabs believed in a creator god called Allah and various lesser deities to whom they turned for help in times of need. The centre of religious life was the Ka'ba in the city of Makkah. The Ka'ba was a stone around which a sanctuary was built. It was said that the gods resided there. Pilgrims from around the peninsula came to worship the deities at the Ka'ba.

Muhammad

Muhammad Born in 570 CE, Muhammad was a member of the Quraish clan (see panel). After being orphaned, he was taken in by his grandfather and then by his uncle Abu Talib, a wealthy merchant. Muhammad grew up to be a trustworthy and hardworking assistant to Abu Talib, and at around the age of 25 he married a wealthy widow named Khadijah.

A spiritual man, Muhammad spent much time in solitude. According to tradition, when he was about 40 years old,

THE QURAISH

In the late sixth century, the Quraish was the dominant clan in Makkah. They controlled the Ka'ba and made money by charging pilgrims a fee for the right to worship at the sacred site. Many people grew resentful of the wealth of the Quraish.

he awoke one night to find himself overpowered by a presence that gripped his body. He found himself speaking the first words of a new scripture in beautiful Arabic poetry. He realized that Allah had chosen

Arabia before the coming of Islam, and the dominant empires of the region.

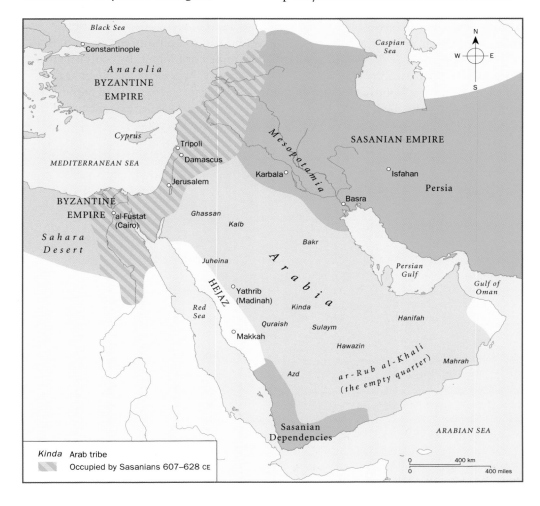

Black Sea

Constantinople

Caspian Sea

Anatolia
BYZANTINE
EMPIRE

N
W   E
S

Cyprus

SASANIAN EMPIRE

MEDITERRANEAN SEA

Tripoli

Damascus

Mesopotamia

Karbala

Isfahan

Persia

Jerusalem

BYZANTINE
EMPIRE   al-Fustat
(Cairo)

Basra

Ghassan

Sahara
Desert

Kalb

Bakr

Arabia

Persian
Gulf

Gulf of
Oman

Juheina

Red
Sea

HEJAZ   Yathrib
(Madinah)

Kinda

Persian
Gulf

Quraish   Sulaym

Hanifah

Makkah

Hawazin

Azd

ar-Rub al-Khali
(the empty quarter)

Mahrah

Sasanian
Dependencies

ARABIAN SEA

Kinda   Arab tribe
▨   Occupied by Sasanians 607–628 CE

0   400 km
0   400 miles

him to be his Prophet, or messenger. After two years of receiving revelations, Muhammad started preaching. He started a new religion called Islam, meaning 'submission' or 'obedience' – submission to the will of God. The Prophet gained followers, who later became known as Muslims (people who follow Islam).

Muhammad's main message was that there is one true God and that after people die, they will be rewarded or punished by God, depending on whether they have led good lives or not. His followers' first duty was therefore to God rather than to their family or tribe. The Prophet taught that all people should be respected, including women and slaves, and that the wealthy should share their riches with the poor.

The Hijrah The wealthy Quraish did not like Muhammad's message. After 619, when Abu Talib died, Muhammad no longer had a protector, and his new community was persecuted in Makkah. In 622, Muhammad and his followers moved to the town of Yathrib. The migration to Yathrib came to be known as the *Hijrah*. Such was the significance of this event in the history of Islam that the year in which it occurred – 622 CE – became year one of the Muslim calendar. Muhammad and his followers were welcomed in Yathrib, and from then on the town was known as Madinat an-Nabi (City of the Prophet), or simply Madinah.

Radical reforms In Madinah, Muhammad implemented many reforms. He created the *ummah*, a new kind of community. To be a member of a traditional community or tribe, a person had to be born into it. By contrast, anyone could join the *ummah* simply by saying the *shahadah*, a profession of faith ('there is no god but Allah, and Muhammad is the messenger of Allah').

THE QUR'AN AND HADITH

Muhammad's followers memorized the revelations he had received. After his death, the revelations were written down to form a book called the Qur'an, which means 'recitation'. The Qur'an contains guidance on lawful and unlawful behaviour for Muslims, as well as stories of the Jewish and Christian prophets who came before Muhammad. It explains the religious duties of a Muslim. During the first century after Muhammad's death, reports of the Prophet's sayings and actions were collated in collections called Hadith.

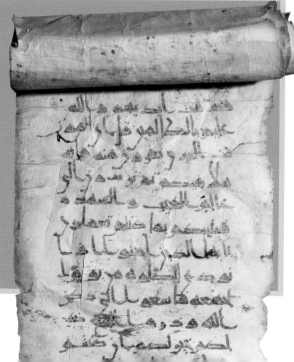

This scroll fragment is from a Qur'an dating from the eighth or ninth century.

Muhammad was the absolute leader of the *ummah*. He declared every person's life equal, so that harming an orphan was as serious as harming a rich man. He outlawed usury since the practice of charging high interest on loans affected the poorest more than the rich. Everyone had to give money to charity, a duty called *zakah*. The amount depended on what people could afford, and the money was distributed to the poor. Muhammad also gave rights to women, such as allowing them to inherit property. The Qur'an says that men should take care of women, but stresses the equality of the sexes in the eyes of Allah:

Allah offers forgiveness and a great
  reward,
For men who surrender to Him, and
  women who surrender to Him,
For men who believe, and women
  who believe,
For men who obey, and women who
  obey,
For men who speak the truth, and
  women who speak the truth…

Qur'an 33:35

The Quraish regarded Muhammad's new society as a threat to their authority and were determined to defeat it. Over the next few years, there were battles between the Quraish, based in Makkah, and the Muslims in Madinah. In 630, the Prophet conquered Makkah and its people accepted his faith. Two years later, Muhammad died. The *ummah* was then ruled in turn by four caliphs (successors): Abu Bakr, Umar, Uthman and Ali. Each of them was appointed by the

Pilgrims during evening prayers at the Prophet's Mosque in Madinah.

THE FIVE PILLARS OF ISLAM

Since the beginning of Islam, Muslims have followed these practices to live a good and responsible life:

1. To state the *shahadah*, the belief in God.
2. To pray five times a day. On Fridays, Muslims gather at the mosque, the place for communal worship.
3. During the Muslim month of Ramadan, to fast during daylight hours.
4. At the end of Ramadan, to give *zakah*, one-fortieth of their wealth, to the poor.
5. To try to make the *hajj* (pilgrimage) to Makkah at least once in their lifetime.

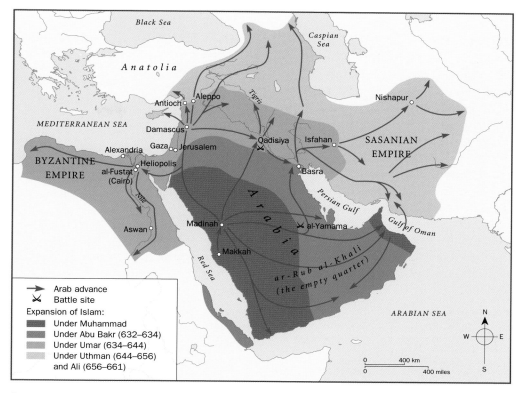

The expansion of Islam under Muhammad and the first four caliphs.

Muslim community. The caliphs rapidly conquered further territory to create an Islamic empire. By 644, the Muslims controlled Arabia, Syria, Palestine, Egypt and the former Persian Empire.

The Umayyads

There was conflict within the *ummah*, however. Uthman (ruled 644–656) was criticized for appointing Umayyads, members of his clan, to important positions. He was assassinated by Muslim soldiers who wanted Ali, Muhammed's son-in-law, to be the new caliph. But not all Muslims accepted Ali's rule. The new Umayyad leader, Muawiyah, opposed Ali, but Ali refused to fight him. This made the rebel group the Kharijites angry and they murdered him in 661. Muawiyah subsequently appointed himself caliph.

Muawiyah established the Umayyad dynasty, which lasted until 750. He ruled the Muslim lands from his new capital in Damascus, Syria. However, the struggle for control of the Islamic empire did not end there. Muawiyah appointed his son Yazid as his successor, but Muslims still loyal to Ali believed that Ali's son Hussain should be caliph. Hussain led a small band of supporters to fight Yazid. In 681, Yazid's vast Umayyad forces surrounded Hussain's group in Karbala (in modern-day Iraq) and massacred virtually all of them.

The Umayyads experienced further rebellion between 683 and 685 from the Shia sect loyal to Ali and the Kharijites, among others. But Abd al-Malik (ruled 685–705) reasserted Umayyad control. He replaced Persian with Arabic as the official language of the empire and introduced Islamic coinage.

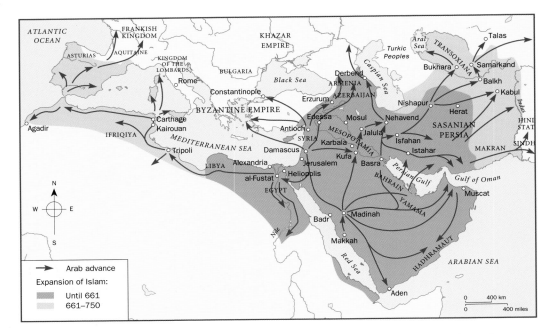

This map shows the continued expansion of the Islamic empire under the Umayyads.

The Dome of the Rock mosque in Jerusalem was completed under the rule of Abd al-Malik. The first major Islamic monument, it was a symbol of confidence in the new religion. Under Abd al-Malik's son, al-Walid I (reigned 705–715), the Umayyad Empire reached its greatest extent. Muslim armies conquered territories beyond the Arabian Peninsula, including Persia (Iran), North Africa and part of Spain.

Debate As the Islamic empire spread, there were debates over its nature. There was disagreement, for example, about the status of non-Arab Muslims. From the beginning of the empire's expansion, the Arab conquerors had kept themselves apart from the subject peoples, living in garrison cities. Non-Arab converts to Islam had inferior status. Yet some Arabs believed that all Muslims should be treated equally, and over time, as most of the

conquered peoples converted to Islam, Arabs and non-Arab Muslims began to intermingle.

A movement to promote Islamic spirituality arose under the preacher Hasan al-Basri (642–728). He advocated a simple lifestyle and taught his followers to meditate on the inner meaning of the Qur'an. This was the start of the mystical Sufism movement (see page 80).

Although al-Basri disagreed with the luxurious lifestyle of the Umayyads, he did not oppose their rule. The Shia, however, maintained that a member of Muhammad's family should reign. The leader of one Shia faction, Abu al-Abbas as-Saffah, claimed descent from the Prophet's uncle. Using this supposed family connection to muster support, he went on to defeat the Umayyads in 750 and proclaim the Abbasid dynasty.

The expansion of Islam By 750, when the Abbasids came to power, the Islamic empire stretched from India to

THE SUNNI–SHIA SPLIT

Two distinct forms developed within Islam. Some Muslims believed that the leadership should remain in the Prophet's family and that Ali should have been the successor to Muhammad (see page 77). They became known as the Shia, the short form of Shiat Ali – 'followers of Ali'. Two of Ali's grandsons survived the massacre in Karbala, and the Shia *imamate* (spiritual leadership) passed down through them. Today, most Shia Muslims believe there have been 12 Imams (leaders) and that the last Imam will return to restore justice on Earth.

The majority of Muslims, however, believed that the leadership should go to the most appropriate person for the job and that Muhammad had not intended to start a dynastic line of rulers. Regarding themselves as the true followers of the Sunnah – the customs of the Prophet – they became known as Sunnis.

Spain. The basis of Abbasid power was their claim that they were the rightful heirs of Muhammad. Once in control, however, the Abbasid rulers increasingly abandoned Muslim principles by living in luxury while most of their subjects remained in poverty. By the time of Caliph Harun al-Rashid (reigned 764–809), the ruler lived in isolation from his subjects at the royal court in Baghdad. The Shia, along with other Muslim groups who hoped to return to the simpler society of the Prophet's time, became increasingly disillusioned.

The Dome of the Rock mosque in Jerusalem displays quotations from the Qur'an proclaiming the unity of God. It was built as a shrine over a rock from which it is believed the Prophet Muhammad rose to heaven.

Abbasid advances Under the Abbasids, the Islamic empire became a major economic power. They encouraged the growth of industry and trade, and there were advances in technology, including the development of papermaking and irrigation. Harun al-Rashid's reign was also a golden age of cultural activity:

SUFISM

Sufism, which began in the eighth century, is the mystical aspect of Islam. Sufis shun worldly wealth and seek an inner, spiritual life. They spend time in contemplation and prayer in order to become closer to God. Since the 12th century, the Sufi movement has been organized in orders (schools), led by Sufi *pirs*, or leaders.

the arts, Arabic grammar, literature and music all flourished. Centres of learning were established throughout the Muslim world, in Egypt, Morocco, Spain, Persia (present-day Iran) and Mesopotamia. The classical texts of the ancient Greek philosophers were translated from Greek and Syriac into Arabic, enabling Muslim scholars to build on learning from the past.

During Abbasid rule, significant progress was made in mathematics, science, astronomy and medicine. For example, the mathematician Al-Khwarizmi (c. 780– c. 850) introduced Arabic numerals and the concept of algebra into European mathematics. The Persian scholar Ibn Sina (980–1037) compiled the *Canon of Medicine*, a vast encyclopaedia of medical knowledge.

Sharia In the eighth century, a comprehensive Islamic code called the *sharia* ('path to be followed') began to be developed. Sharia law was based on the Qur'an and the Sunnah. During the ninth and tenth centuries, Muslim rulers encouraged leading scholars to write down the law. Five schools of law were named after the learned men who initiated them – four Sunni scholars and one Shia. Sharia law contains rules for organizing society as well as governing the behaviour

Sufi mystics from Pakistan. The Sufis helped to spread Islam throughout the world. They played an important role in educating people and reinforcing the spiritual aspect of the religion.

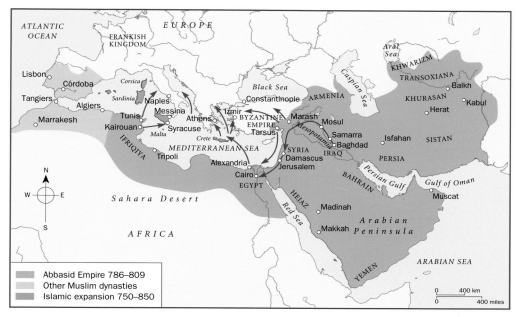

The Abbasid Empire in 850. By this time, several different Islamic dynasties were in existence.

of individuals towards each other and in relation to God. Many Muslim rulers developed an additional legal system that helped them in the day-to-day needs of government, especially to deal with matters of crime, property disputes and commerce.

A divided empire

Although the Abbasid dynasty lasted until 1258, by the 10th century their rulers were unable to command authority over all the Muslim lands. The Buyids from Persia took control of the empire's capital, Baghdad, in 945 and ruled western Persia and Mesopotamia until 1055. The Abbasid caliph remained the symbolic head of the empire, but its regions were ruled by independent regimes, including the Caliphate of Córdoba in Spain and the Fatimid Empire in Egypt.

The Caliphate of Córdoba

A Muslim army first entered Spain from North Africa in 711 and established an Islamic kingdom that became known as Al-Andalus, in the south and centre of the Iberian Peninsula. Muslim rule in Spain changed dramatically following the collapse of the Umayyads. When the Abbasids took power in Baghdad in 750, they massacred members of the Umayyad clan to secure control. One Umayyad prince, Abd ar-Rahman, escaped and made his way to Spain. In 756, he initiated a new Umayyad dynasty there, the Caliphate of Córdoba.

By the 10th century, Córdoba, the capital of Al-Andalus, with clean, paved streets, running water and 70 libraries, was one of the world's most advanced cities. Its Great Mosque was an impressive architectural feat. The Muslim rulers allowed Christians and Jews to practise their religion and to work and study freely, enabling an interchange of ideas and learning between the scholars of different faiths. As a result, Córdoba became a major centre of culture and scholarship.

Between the 11th and 13th centuries, Al-Andalus was controlled in turn by two Muslim dynasties from North Africa: the Almoravids (1056–1147) and the Almohads (1130–1269). During this period, the Christian rulers of northern Spain fought to reconquer the region. After centuries of struggle, the Christians achieved their aim, and Muslim rule ended in 1492.

The Fatimids The Shia caliphate of the Fatimids was established in Tunisia, North Africa, when Abdallah al-Mahdi took power, claiming to be a descendant of Fatima, a daughter of Muhammad, and her husband Ali. In 972, the Fatimids moved their capital to Cairo in Egypt. At its height, in the mid-11th century, the Fatimid Empire ruled North Africa, Egypt, Syria, Palestine and much of Arabia. It subsequently fell into decline, owing to the growing power of the Saljuk Turks.

IBN RUSHD (1126–1198)

The writings of Spanish Muslim scholars had a significant influence in Europe. Among the most influential was Ibn Rushd, who had trained in Islamic law, medicine and philosophy. He became chief *qadi* (judge) of Córdoba (see page 81). In the 1150s or 1160s, he was asked by the Almohad caliph, Abu Yaqub Yusuf, to provide a correct interpretation of the Greek philosopher Aristotle. He presented Aristotle's thought clearly, helping readers to understand it. Ibn Rushd's work remained influential in Europe and the Islamic world for centuries after his death.

A portrait of Ibn Rushd. Few translated works of Aristotle existed in Europe before he translated them into Latin and enabled scholars to study these important ancient texts once again.

JIHAD

The word *jihad* is Arabic for 'to strive' or 'to struggle'. It refers to all the ways in which people try to serve God. Jihad is the effort that people make in their lives to act in accordance with God's wishes. It can also mean striving to spread Islam and to defend Muslims from aggressors, which may involve war.

The Prophet was asked about people fighting because they are brave, or in honour of a certain loyalty, or to show off: which of them fights for the cause of Allah? He replied, 'The person who struggles so that Allah's word is supreme is the one serving Allah's cause.'

Hadith

The Saljuks

In 1055, the Saljuk Turks (a dynasty that had converted to Islam in the 990s) seized power from the Buyids in Baghdad. The Abbasid caliph crowned their leader sultan, the new title used by Muslim rulers. The Saljuks agreed to uphold Islamic law and defend Islam from its enemies. Under the Saljuks, local military governors ruled each district of the empire (which included a large part of Central Asia, Persia, Mesopotamia, Syria and Palestine), along with the Muslim clergy, the *ulama*, whose authority came from the Qur'an. Religious schools called *madrasas* were set up across the empire to provide formal training for the *ulama*. The *ulama* took charge of the legal system through the sharia courts, giving them considerable power in their local area.

The Crusades

The Saljuks' commitment to defend Islam was soon put to the test. In 1071, they were attacked near Manzikert (in modern Turkey) by an army of the Christian Byzantine Empire. Although they were victorious in the battle, by the end of the century the Saljuk Empire had become divided and weak. It was at this time of Muslim disunity that Pope Urban II, head of the Roman Catholic Church, gave a sermon that inspired the Crusades, a series of military expeditions from Europe that attempted to halt the spread of Islam and win back the Holy Land (Palestine).

The ruins of Qalat al-Gundi, a fort built in the Sinai desert in Egypt by Salah ad-Din as protection against the crusaders and to guard the pilgrimage routes to Makkah.

In 1099, Christian crusaders from western Europe attacked Jerusalem. Already a sacred city for Christians and Jews, Jerusalem was also the third holiest city in the Islamic world after Makkah and Madinah. It was the site of the Dome of the Rock mosque, which was where Muslims believe Muhammad ascended to heaven. The crusaders succeeded in

MANSA MUSA (1307–1332)

The best-known West African Muslim ruler of the Middle Ages was the king of Mali, Mansa Musa. After making the pilgrimage to Makkah in 1324–1325, he built magnificent mosques, libraries and *madrasas* throughout his empire to encourage Islamic learning. Arab traveller Ibn Battutah admired the people of Mali for learning the Qur'an, noting how 'They put their children in chains if they show any backwardness in memorizing it, and they are not set free until they have it by heart.'

conquering Jerusalem and established Christian states in Palestine, Lebanon and Anatolia (part of modern-day Turkey).

In 1171, a Kurdish general named Salah ad-Din overthrew the Fatimid dynasty in Egypt. Between 1174 and 1186, he united the Muslim territories of Syria, northern Mesopotamia and Palestine under his leadership, and proceeded to lead a jihad, or struggle, against the crusaders. Salah ad-Din recaptured Jerusalem in 1187 and founded his own dynasty, the Ayyubids.

A mosque in Djenné, which was a thriving town under the Mali Empire. Several examples of Islamic architecture from that time can still be seen there today.

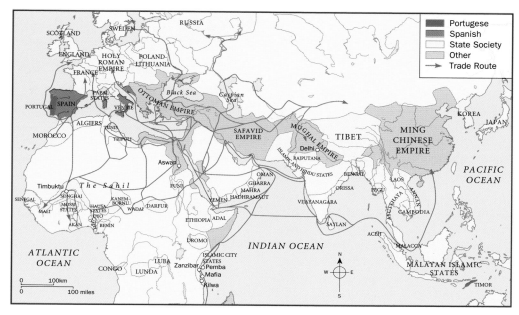

A map showing world trade routes and empires in around 1500.

Africa Islam did not expand through war and conquest alone. Muslim traders helped to spread Islam to far-flung regions, distant from the Islamic heartlands, including East and West Africa. In the seventh century, Arab conquerors reached Aswan in Egypt and continued to move southwards into East Africa. The Funj dynasty in modern-day Sudan converted to Islam in the 16th century. The region was close to Arabia and so the Arab influence was strong. Arab and Persian traders and settlers mixed with the local people, giving rise to a new culture – Swahili. The Swahili language, for example, mixes the African language Bantu with Arabic words, and is written using the Arabic alphabet.

In West Africa, the spread of Islam was mostly peaceful, and Islamic customs merged with local practices. Trading links had already developed between the Maghreb (present-day Morocco) and the Sahil (the area between the Sahara Desert and the tropical forests of Guinea) before the seventh century. From the mid-600s, when North Africa became part of the Islamic empire, merchants took the ideas of Islam with them on their trading expeditions southwards. Many West African royal families converted voluntarily to the new religion, which they believed gave them prestige. They funded religious scholarships to further increase their status. Timbuktu on the River Niger became the most important centre of Islamic culture in Africa.

Indian Ocean The Islamic empire also took control of the trade routes in the Indian Ocean. By 1500, Muslim merchants were trading with those in India, China, the Malacca Islands and beyond, prompting Muslim communities to develop in these places. There is evidence of Muslims having settled on the islands of Pemba, Zanzibar, Mafia and Kilwa between 1000 and 1150. The Arab traveller Ibn Battuta (c. 1304–c. 1377) also discovered Muslim communities along the southern coastline of China.

India Islam first appeared in India in 711 when the Arabs invaded Sindh (in modern-day south-eastern Pakistan). The conquest of the Indian subcontinent began with the Ghurids, an Islamic dynasty of Persian (Iranian) descent, who occupied northern India in the late 12th century. An independent sultanate was formed in Delhi that lasted from 1206 to 1526.

Some of the early Muslim rulers destroyed Hindu temples and replaced them with large mosques to show their dominance. However, a tolerant religious policy was established under the Tughluq dynasty (1320–1413). As much as 20 to 25 per cent of the population of the Delhi Sultanate (which by the mid-1300s covered all of India except for the southern tip and the west coast) may have converted to Islam, while the rest remained Hindu. Those who did convert combined Islamic practices with local Hindu rituals – Hinduism is a religion that readily incorporates other religious practices (see Chapter 4).

The Mamluks From around 900, it was common for Muslim rulers to buy slaves to fight as warriors in their armies. They were known as *mamluks*. Once freed, the mamluks were sometimes able to rise in society and some even became rulers. It was mamluk soldiers who put an end to Salah ad-Din's Ayyubid dynasty in 1250.

The Mamluks proclaimed their own sultanate and initiated a period of rule that lasted until about 1500. Based in Cairo, they demonstrated their devotion to Islam by funding the Sufi orders and Islamic scholarship, and constructing elaborate mosques. However, in 1517 the Mamluk era came to an end, defeated by the Ottomans.

The Mongols Meanwhile, in Mongolia, a new empire was emerging.

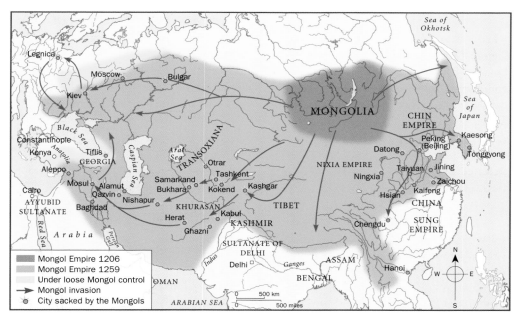

The Mongol invasions of the 13th century. The Mongols' knowledge of the latest warfare techniques enabled them to wreak destruction on a huge scale.

Whirling Dervishes in the dance hall in Rumi's adopted home town of Konya in Turkey, where he died. The mosque, dance hall and tombs of leaders of his Sufi order still attract pilgrims today.

Founded in the 13th century by the ruthless leader Genghis Khan (c. 1162–1227), by 1259 the Mongol Empire stretched from northern China in the East to what is now Germany in the West. After Genghis Khan's death, his descendants created several separate Mongol states that sometimes fought each other as well as other peoples. In their early conquests, the Mongols inflicted massive destruction on their enemies. They ravaged cities, killing entire populations. In 1258, the Mongols defeated the Abbasid caliphate and sacked Baghdad. It took them 40 days to execute all the inhabitants of the city.

In the years that followed, Hülegü, leader of one of the Mongol states, converted to Islam, and by the beginning of the 14th century, all the western Mongol states had followed his example. The Mongols began to rebuild the cities they had razed and became patrons of the arts, sciences, mathematics and history.

RUMI (1207–1273)

The Sufi mystic and poet Jalal ad-Din ar-Rumi lived through the destruction of the Mongol invasions. In about 1218, Rumi and his family fled their native city of Khurasan in eastern Persia (Iran) and made their way to Konya in Anatolia. Rumi's experience led him to initiate a mystical movement, which helped people come to terms with the disaster. After his death, his followers formed the Sufi Mevlevi order. Often known as the Whirling Dervishes, its members performed a spinning dance in order to enter a trance and become one with God. Rumi composed some 30,000 verses and many *robaiyat* (a form of Iranian poetry).

> *As salt resolved in the ocean*
> *I was swallowed in God's sea,*
> *Past faith, past unbelieving,*
> *Past doubt, past certainty.*
>
> *Suddenly in my bosom*
> *A star shone clear and bright;*
> *All the suns of heaven*
> *Vanished in that star's light.*

The Robaiyat of Jalal ad-Din ar-Rumi: Select Translations into English Verse by A J Arberry, 1949

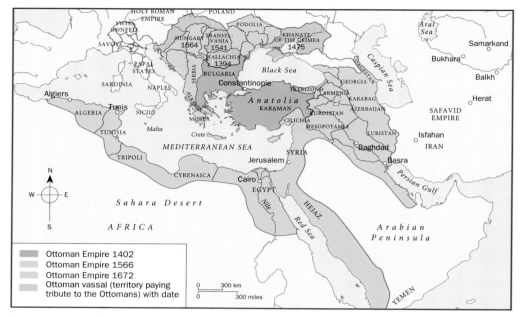

This map shows the rise of the Ottoman Empire (1328–1672) – the most far-reaching Islamic empire.

Timur Lane By the mid-14th century, the Mongol states were in decline. Mongol general Timur Lane (c. 1336–1405) attempted to reverse this change in fortunes. He conquered much of Central Asia, Mesopotamia and Persia (Iran), as well as the cities of Delhi in India and Ankara in modern-day Turkey. Under Timur and his successors, Herat, Samarkand and Bukhara (all in Central Asia) became magnificent cities. Timur made Samarkand his capital. He brought in craftsmen from all over the empire to construct the city and invited scholars, artists and historians to settle and develop it as a centre of Islamic culture. Although he belonged to the Sunni sect, Timur also offered Shias protection under his rule.

The Ottomans As the Mongol states were declining, the Ottomans – a Turkish tribe – were establishing an empire in Anatolia. By 1400, the Ottomans had conquered Serbia, Bulgaria and most of the Byzantine Empire. In 1453, the Ottoman ruler Sultan Mehmet II captured the Byzantine city of Constantinople, which he renamed Istanbul. The empire continued to expand. By the mid-1500s, the Ottomans had conquered most of Hungary and had taken control of a vast area of Europe stretching from the Crimea to southern Greece. They also conquered a large swathe of the Islamic lands during the 16th century, including eastern Anatolia, northern Mesopotamia, Syria, Yemen and most of North Africa.

The Ottoman Empire was able to expand largely because of its effective army. Like other Muslim rulers, the Ottomans used slave soldiers. Their elite troops were the Janissaries. Taken from Christian families as boys, they were converted to Islam and trained as soldiers. As they were outsiders and totally dependent on the sultan for their position, the Janissaries were fiercely loyal to their ruler.

The Ottomans maintained a firm grip on their empire. It was divided into provinces, each ruled by a *pasha* (general) who was directly responsible to the sultan. The sultan appointed *qadis* to run the justice system based on sharia law, which became the official law for all Muslims. The Ottomans brought the *ulama* (see page 83) under their control. The *ulama* provided religious leadership and helped the people to accept Ottoman rule.

Many different religious and ethnic groups lived within the empire, including Christians, Arabs, Jews, Berbers (native North Africans) and Turks. Although the sultan exerted strong religious control over Muslims through sharia law, he allowed other communities to follow their own customs, and it was possible for non-Muslims to achieve high rank within the empire. However, the Ottomans had a different attitude towards the peoples outside their empire. They saw themselves as defenders of Islam against its enemies. As Sunni Muslims, not only did they fight the Christians to the West, but also the Shia Safavids to the east.

The Suleimaniye mosque in Istanbul was the largest mosque ever built in the Ottoman Empire. Sinan adapted the Hagia Sophia church design to include large open spaces where Muslims could pray together.

THE SULEIMANIYE MOSQUE

Under Sultan Suleiman the Magnificent (reigned 1520–1566), Ottoman culture reached its height. He patronized art, history, medicine and architecture. One of his crowning achievements was the Suleimaniye mosque in Istanbul, constructed to rival the Hagia Sophia church (built 537 CE). The architect Sinan based the general layout of the mosque on the design of the Hagia Sophia. Built in the 1550s, the mosque had four minaret towers. Within the complex were a *madrasa*, a hospital, a dining hall, a *caravanserai* (inn for travellers), baths, hospices and shops.

The Safavids The founder of the Safavid Empire, Shah Ismail, conquered Tabriz in 1501, and over the next ten years also took control of the rest of Persia (Iran) and the Iraqi provinces of Baghdad and Mosul. Although most of the population were Sunni, Shah Ismail declared Shia Islam to be the religion of his empire. This brought it into conflict with the Sunni Ottomans. In 1514, the Ottoman ruler Selim I (1467–1520) defeated the Safavids at the Battle of Chaldiran and went on to gain control of eastern Anatolia.

Later that century, however, the Safavid ruler Shah Abbas I (1571–1629) achieved significant victories against the Ottomans. He strengthened Shia Islam within his empire by bringing in Shia *ulama* from other countries and building Shia madrasas. He introduced annual rituals to mourn the death of the Prophet's grandson Hussain at Karbala. A procession of mourners expressed an emotional outpouring of grief, as if Hussain had been killed only recently. Grieving for Hussain became central to religious life, and Shia Islam became important to Persian national identity.

Under Shah Abbas' reign, the capital, Isfahan, became a cultural centre. The art of Persian miniature painting flourished, and the city was filled with elaborate

The courtyard and pool of the Imam (Shah) mosque in Isfahan, Iran.

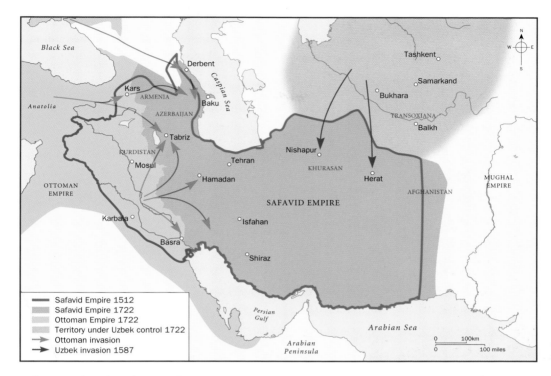

The Safavid Empire. The map shows the invasions that weakened the empire.

palaces and parks, along with great mosques and madrasas. Yet by the late 17th century, the empire was in decline. After 1748, when Shah Nadir Khan was assassinated, the central government collapsed in Persia (present-day Iran). A period of anarchy followed, with Ottomans and Russians controlling the north and various tribal chiefs competing for power in the south. The *ulama*, however, retained the loyalty and religious devotion of the Persian people. In 1779, when a new dynasty, the Qajars, seized control of Persia, the *ulama* retained their important position.

MUSLIM SHRINES

Shrines with images of saints have always played an important role in the Islamic culture of India, unlike in other Muslim countries where the use of images in worship is discouraged. Shrines dedicated to the memory of the great Sufi saints were established at tombs. Seen as a gateway to God, attendants would carry out daily rituals at the shrines, washing and decorating them.

The shrine at the tomb of Muslim saint Khajwa Moinudin Chisti, at Ajmer, is one such example. It includes a magnificent mosque built by the Mughal emperor Shah Jahan. For the Muslims of India it is considered the next most important holy place after Makkah and Madinah.

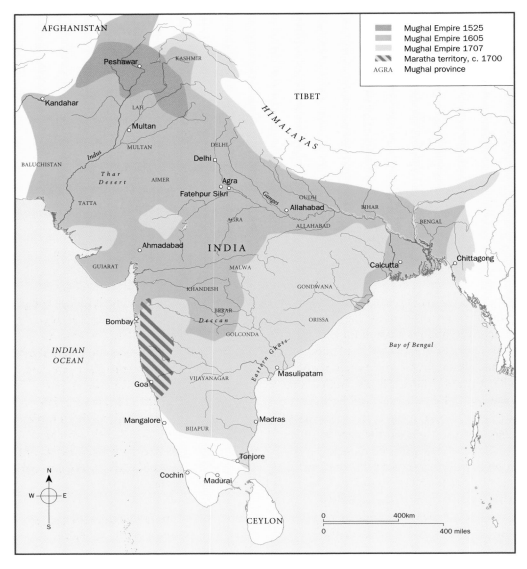

The following labels appear on the map:

AFGHANISTAN

Mughal Empire 1525
Mughal Empire 1605
Mughal Empire 1707
Maratha territory, c. 1700
AGRA Mughal province

Peshawar KASHMIR

TIBET

Kandahar LAH

Multan

HIMALAYAS

MULTAN DELHI

Indus

BALUCHISTAN

Thar
Desert AJMER Delhi

Agra
Fatehpur Sikri Ganges OUDH

TATTA AGRA Allahabad BIHAR

ALLAHABAD BENGAL

Ahmadabad INDIA

Chittagong

GUJARAT MALWA Calcutta

KHANDESH GONDWANA

BERAR Deccan ORISSA

Bombay

GOLCONDA

INDIAN
OCEAN Bay of Bengal

VIJAYANAGAR Eastern Ghats Masulipatam

Goa

Mangalore Madras

BIJAPUR

Tonjore

N Cochin Madurai

W — E

S CEYLON

0   400km
0   400 miles

The Mughals

The Mughal emperors in India were Sunni Muslims. In 1526, the first Mughal emperor, Babur (1483–1530), conquered Delhi and paved the way for the conquest of northern India. His grandson Akbar (1556–1605) extended Mughal power over most of the country. Akbar proved a tolerant ruler, respectful of all faiths. He abolished the tax that non-Muslims had been forced to pay, which had been imposed by Muslim rulers in all their conquered territories since the

The expansion of the Mughal Empire throughout India between 1526 and 1707.

seventh century. Akbar became a vegetarian and gave up hunting in order not to offend Hindus. He also built Hindu temples and founded a house of worship where scholars of all religions could meet and debate.

The Sufi orders helped to spread Islam in India. The Sufi pirs (spiritual leaders, or living saints) won converts from tribal peoples and the lower Hindu castes – people who were disadvantaged under the

WALI ALLAH AND THE REFORMIST MOVEMENT

Wali Allah (1702/3–1762), who grew up during the period of Mughal decline, became one of the leaders of an Islamic reformist movement. He believed that to revive Islamic power, Indian Muslims should become unified and strengthen links with the rest of the Muslim world. They should not follow other Indian traditions, but should return to a more traditional form of Islamic practice, stripped of such Indian adaptations as the worship of saints. The reformist message appealed to educated Muslims, but had less impact among the larger numbers of poorer Muslims, who continued to worship at shrines and enjoy lively popular festivals.

Hindu social system. The pirs used local languages to teach the message of Islam.

Akbar's grandson, Shah Jahan (reigned 1628–1658), further extended Mughal power. Known for the splendour of his court and his passion for building, Shah Jahan commissioned the famous Taj Mahal, a monument to the memory of his wife, Mumtaz Mahal. He also built a huge palace in Delhi called the Red Fort, and the Jami' Masjid in Agra, one of the most spectacular mosques in the country.

Shah Jahan was relatively tolerant of Hinduism, but his son Shah Aurangzeb (reigned 1658–1707) ordered the destruction of many Hindu temples, reintroduced the tax payable by non-Muslims, and banned Shia Muslims from holding celebrations in memory of Hussain. He forbade the drinking of wine and prohibited music at court. These policies accorded with the growing reformist movement (see panel above).

Aurangzeb's religious intolerance provoked major revolts against the regime, and the Mughal Empire began to weaken. Hindu and Sikh rulers conquered parts of northern India. In 1739, the Persian ruler Nadir Shah invaded northern India and sacked Delhi. The British, who had entered India as traders, took advantage of Mughal decline and began to take control of the Indian states.

The best-known monument in India, the Taj Mahal.

Ottoman weakness The

Ottoman Empire also began its decline in the late 17th century. Like the other Islamic empires, the economy of the Ottoman Empire was based largely on agriculture and long-established trading relationships, and lacked the opportunity for further expansion. By contrast, the economies of Europe's major powers grew rapidly between the 17th and 19th centuries due to the opening up of trade with the Americas and East Asia, as well as technological advances that led to large-scale industrialization. In the late 17th and the 18th centuries, the Ottomans lost territory to European powers, including the Habsburgs, the Venetians, the Poles and the Russians. The Ottoman Empire gradually broke up and eventually collapsed in the early 1920s.

Islam around the world As

the empires of the Safavids, Mughals and Ottomans waned, Islam flourished in other parts of the world. From around 1500, Islam came to South-East Asia, establishing itself through trade rather than conquest. The first major Muslim state in this region was founded in Aceh in northern Sumatra in around 1524. Macassar and Mataram became Muslim states in the early 17th century. As in India, Sufi teachers, some of whom were also merchants, presented Islamic teachings in a way that Hindus could understand. Consequently Islamic customs frequently intermingled with the local traditions of Hinduism and animism.

West Africa In the 18th and 19th

centuries, a series of *jihad* movements in West Africa led to the establishment of a number of Islamic states. The leaders of these movements were generally *ulama* who had studied with Sufi masters and preached a reformist version of Islam. The most famous jihad leader was Uthman Dan Fodio who, in the early 19th century, set up the sultanate of Sokoto (see panel).

The jihad movements appealed to the poor and discontented in those societies, such as runaway slaves. They were also supported by the cattle herders of the Fulani tribe (living in present-day Nigeria

Abubakar Sidiq, former Sultan of Sokoto, ruled the Sokoto Caliphate from 1938 to 1988. After Sokoto was brought under British control in 1903, the role became increasingly ceremonial, although the Sultan still has influence over the Fulani and Hausa peoples of northern Nigeria.

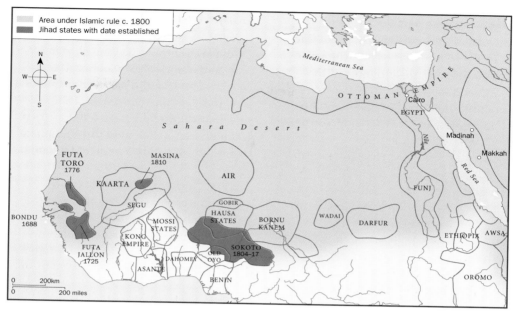

Area under Islamic rule c. 1800
Jihad states with date established

The jihad states in around 1800, and the extent of Islam in West Africa at the time.

and other West African countries), who were unhappy about the taxes imposed by local kings. One Fulani scholar called Ibrahim Musa fought local rulers and, in 1725, set up an Islamic state called Futa Jallon (in present-day Guinea).

India The rapid expansion of the European economies from the 18th century onwards had a disastrous impact on the Islamic world. European countries needed new markets, so they conquered large areas of the Muslim world in North Africa, the Middle East and Asia and set up colonies there in order to draw them into their trade networks.

UTHMAN DAN FODIO (1754–1817)

A Muslim scholar and teacher, Uthman Dan Fodio came from the Hausa kingdom of Gobir (north-western Nigeria). During the 1780s and 1790s he established a reputation as a religious and political leader. He gained support from the Hausa peasants, who believed he was the Mahdi, in Shia tradition the 12th Imam who would return to the world to restore justice. In 1802, a conflict arose between Dan Fodio's community and the rulers of Gobir, so he decided to make a hijrah (see page 75) to Gudu, 48 kilometres to the north, where he became the imam. He set up a caliphate based on the simple social justice of the Prophet's community in Madinah. Soon afterwards, Dan Fodio raised an army and launched a jihad (see page 83) against the Hausa rulers. By 1808, he had overthrown most of the Hausa kingdoms to form the sultanate of Sokoto. It expanded over the following two decades to include most of present-day northern Nigeria and the northern Cameroons. After the success of the jihad, Dan Fodio retired from public life.

There were frequent challenges to colonial rule. In British-controlled India in 1857, Bengali Muslim soldiers in the British Army erupted in mutiny upon

THE SALAFIYYAH MOVEMENT

To achieve Muslim unity and restore the spiritual strength of Islam, Muhammad Abdu believed Muslims should return to the principles of social justice practised by the early community. But he also thought that these principles should be adjusted to fit with modern democratic values. All sources of Muslim law, including the Qur'an and the Sunnah (the customs of the Prophet), should be open to debate by all Muslims. It should be possible to change an Islamic law in accordance with modern requirements. He said: 'If a ruling has become the cause of harm which it did not cause before, then we must change it according to the prevailing [current] conditions.'

discovering that the army used beef and pork fat to grease the rifle cartridges. (This practice was offensive to Hindus, who consider cows to be sacred, and to Muslims, for whom pigs are unclean.) As well as expressing their anger at colonial policies that were draining the country of its natural resources, Muslims feared that their faith and culture were under attack.

Egypt In Egypt, which fell under British control in 1882, the British took over cotton production and built ports, railways and the Suez Canal to help them transport goods and manage the economy. Taxes for local people rose dramatically to fund these massive projects (although Europeans living in Egypt paid very little tax). There was widespread resistance to this policy and other aspects of colonial rule. The Islamic reform movements became involved in the Egyptian resistance. Influential reformers Muhammad Abdu (1849–1905) and Jamal ad-Din al-Afghani (1838–1897) initiated the Salafiyyah movement (see panel). As a response to European domination, they promoted the idea of pan-Islamism – Muslim unity across national boundaries.

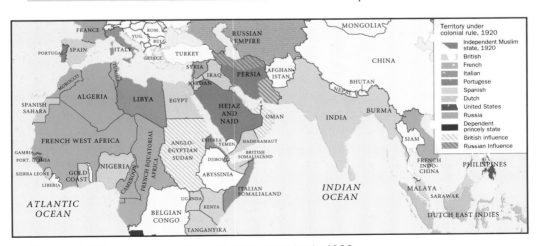

The extent of European control over Muslim countries in 1920.

A contemporary European illustration portraying Indians fighting British soldiers during the Siege of Lucknow, northern India, in July 1857.

In the early 20th century, a new generation of Muslim reformers arose, led by the Egyptian Hasan al-Banna (1906–1949). In 1928, al-Banna founded the Society of the Muslim Brothers (the Muslim Brotherhood), an Islamic movement for social justice. Al-Banna had witnessed British colonists living in luxury while Egyptian workers were in poverty. To him, this was a religious problem. An Islamic government, in control of the religious, economic, social and cultural life of the country, would therefore be the solution. Al-Banna believed that Muslims must make a jihad to reform society and that the Qur'an should be interpreted to meet the requirements of modern life, including the struggle for social justice.

Not only did the Brothers train their followers in Muslim beliefs, they also built clinics and hospitals and set up factories where workers received fair pay. The majority of members accepted that social welfare was a vital part of spreading the Islamic way of life; a minority attempted to achieve their aims through terrorism. The ideas of the Muslim Brothers spread throughout the Middle East.

Hasan al-Banna explained the mission of the Muslim Brothers in a document entitled 'Between Yesterday and Today':

Brethren, recall that more than 60 per cent of the Egyptians live at a subhuman level, that they get enough to eat only through the most arduous toil, and Egypt is threatened by murderous famines and exposed to many economic problems of which only Allah can know the outcome. Recall too that there are more than 320 foreign companies in Egypt, monopolizing all public utilities and all important facilities in every part of the country…. Among your aims are to work for the reform of education; to war against poverty, ignorance, disease, and crime; and to create an exemplary society which will deserve to be associated with the Islamic Sacred Law.

Muslims under French rule

French colonialism differed from British colonialism since the French were encouraged to settle in their country's colonies. After France conquered Algeria, Morocco and Tunisia in the 19th century, they handed over land to French and other European settlers. By 1940, settlers occupied 35–40 per cent of the farmland in Algeria. The French also had a policy of assimilation, wanting their colonies to adopt French culture. Under French rule, Muslim culture was accordingly suppressed and traditional Islamic colleges were abolished or had their money seized. In the 1920s and 1930s, Islamic reformers in Algeria joined with nationalists to fight for independence from France, which they eventually won in 1962.

Saudi Arabia Unlike many other Muslim countries, Arabia was not colonized. In the mid-18th century, an Arabian prince named Muhammad Ibn Saud made an alliance with Muhammad al-Wahhab, an extreme Muslim reformer.

After conquering Makkah and Madinah, they set fire to all books except the Qur'an. They also banned music and flowers from the holy cities, and the use of tobacco and coffee. Men were forced to grow beards, and women had to be veiled and remain separate from men. Al-Wahhab's religious ideas later became known in the West as Wahhabism and as Islamic fundamentalism.

In the early 1900s, one of Ibn Saud's descendants conquered the entire lands of Arabia. In 1932, he proclaimed the foundation of the Kingdom of Saudi Arabia and became King Abd al-Aziz Ibn Saud. The Saudis claimed to be the heirs of pure Islam. They declared they would rule in the same way as the Muslims of the seventh century, following the Qur'an. Medieval punishments, such as cutting off the hand of a thief, became part of Saudi

Algerian boys cleaning the boots of French soldiers in 1960. France had granted independence to Morocco and Tunisia in 1956, but Algerians were still waging a struggle for freedom from colonial rule.

Nearly one million pilgrims face the Ka'ba during sunset prayers at the Great Mosque in Makkah.

law. Yet some of these laws, such as the banning of alcohol and gambling, did not in fact exist in the Prophet's time.

Most Muslim organizations disagreed with this interpretation of Islam, including the Muslim Brothers. They also believed it was against Quranic values for Saudi Arabia's rulers to live in great luxury while most of the population lived in poverty. Nevertheless, Saudi Arabia remained significant to Muslims worldwide as the birthplace of Islam and their spiritual home. Pilgrims came in large numbers to visit the sacred sites to fulfill the hajj, the fifth pillar of Islam.

Another point of conflict among Muslims has been the strong connection between Saudi Arabia and Western countries, particularly the USA. Oil was discovered in the kingdom in the 1930s, and the American Standard Oil Company helped found a new company to enable the Saudis to extract their oil. Control of

THE HAJJ

The *hajj*, or pilgrimage to Makkah, has been performed in Arabia for centuries. Since Muhammad's time, pilgrimage rituals have been linked to events in his life, as well as to earlier deeds related in the Bible. The purpose of the hajj is to stop all worldly activities for a short time in order to focus on God alone. It involves a number of rituals, including circling the Ka'ba in Makkah seven times and kissing the Black Stone in the wall of the Ka'ba. Pilgrims must also travel back and forth seven times between the hills of Safa and Marwah in memory of Hagar (the prophet Ibrahim's wife) and her search for water for her child, Ismail, the forefather of the Arabs. They visit the plain of Arafat where Muhammad preached his final sermon. On the final day, they hold a feast to remember how Ibrahim was willing to sacrifice his son for God.

the oil industry made the USA the most influential foreign nation in Saudi Arabia, but many Muslims were uneasy about an Islamic country having such close ties with the West.

EXTREMISM IN INDIA

Extremist Hindu organizations, such as the Bharatiya Janata Party (BJP), want to end secular (non-religious) rule in India and establish Hinduism as the country's religion. In 1992, militant Hindus stormed the Ayodhya mosque in northern India and destroyed it, shouting 'Hindustan [the Indian subcontinent] is for the Hindus' and 'Death to Muslims'. The destruction of the mosque sparked some of the worst violence between Hindus and Muslims since Partition. In a cycle of revenge attacks, Muslims attacked temples and Hindus ransacked mosques. Around 2,000 people lost their lives in the riots. More recently, extreme Islamic groups in some locations have carried out attacks on Hindus. For instance, in 2002, a group of Muslims attacked a train carrying Hindu pilgrims.

Independence and Islam
Most colonies with large Muslim populations gained their independence from European rule after World War II. In some cases, such as India and Palestine, decolonization increased the divisions between religious groups, leading to bloodshed. Some

Muslim countries, such as Egypt, tried to separate religion from the state to create modern, Western-style nations. But people became disillusioned with these attempts when their governments failed to raise living standards. Many Muslims became supporters of Communism, as practised in the Soviet Union. Others looked to their faith for a solution, and a small minority joined radical Islamic movements.

India On gaining its independence from Britain in 1947, India was partitioned: most of India was Hindu, while the new state of Pakistan (split into East Pakistan and West Pakistan) was mostly Muslim. As soon as the new borders of the countries were known, around ten million people fled their homes across the border

India 1992: residents of Ayodhya sift through the rubble of their mosque after it was destroyed by Hindu extremists.

to the country where they hoped to be safe. Muslims in India rushed to Pakistan while Hindus and Sikhs fled in the opposite direction. Hundreds of thousands of people were murdered in ferocious religious massacres. The tensions between India and Pakistan continue to this day. The two countries are in dispute over the territory of Kashmir, which became divided during Partition. India and Pakistan fought two wars over Kashmir, in 1947–48 and 1965. A further war, in 1971, resulted in East Pakistan becoming a separate nation, Bangladesh.

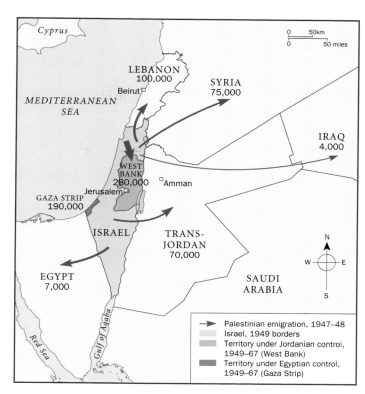

This map shows the dispersal of Palestinians to neighbouring lands during the conflict of 1947–48. The majority remain refugees to this day.

HOLY SITES IN JERUSALEM

The city of Jerusalem, which has been under full Israeli control since the Arab-Israeli war of 1967, contains sites holy to Judaism, Islam and Christianity. The most significant Jewish site is the Western Wall of the Temple Mount, regarded as the only remaining part of the Second Jewish Temple, which was destroyed in 70 CE. The Temple Mount, known in Arabic as Haram al-Sharif, also has two major Muslim shrines – the Dome of the Rock and the Al-Aqsa Mosque. For Christians, the Church of the Holy Sepulchre marks the place where Jesus was killed and has been an important pilgrimage destination since the fourth century.

The Arab-Israeli conflict

As in India, the roots of the conflict between the mostly Muslim Arabs and the Jewish Israelis lie in colonial times. For an account of the conflict, the establishment of the State of Israel, and the dispersion of hundreds of thousands of Palestinians to their current locations in the West Bank and Gaza Strip, see pages 32–35. The Palestinian refugees have never given up the political struggle to regain their homeland. A minority have resorted to violent attacks, to which Israel has responded with force. The conflict continues to this day.

Islamic radicals

Since World War II a number of Islamic movements within Muslim countries have pressed for a return to what they see as fundamental Islamic principles and government based on sharia law. Most have been prepared to operate under existing governments, setting up mosques and welfare societies to show that Islam can work for the people. However, a minority of radical Islamic movements, such as in Egypt and Algeria, have claimed that their countries are not truly Islamic and have used violence to try to take power.

These Islamist movements were inspired by the ideas of the Egyptian writer Sayyid Qutb (1906–1966), a member of the Muslim Brotherhood (see page 97). In 1952, Gamal Abdel Nasser seized power in Egypt and established a secular government. He persecuted the Muslim Brotherhood, imprisoning Qutb for being a member of this organization in 1956. Qutb argued that although Nasser claimed he was a Muslim, the country was not ruled on an Islamic basis. Egypt, he said, was in a state of 'barbarism', like pre-Islamic Arabia. Muslims were therefore duty bound to overthrow the government.

Qutb called on Muslims to model themselves on Muhammad. They should separate themselves from mainstream society and dedicate themselves to violent jihad. (In fact, the Prophet Muhammad preached a message of tolerance and opposed the use of force in religious matters.) Qutb's ideas influenced all the Sunni Islamist movements.

Iran

In some countries, Islamist movements have succeeded in taking power. In Iran, Shah Muhammad Reza Pahlavi (ruled 1949–1979) modernized the country economically, but banned political parties and his secret police crushed any opposition. The shah was overthrown in a popular revolution in 1978–79, and a religious leader named Ayatollah Khomeini took power. Khomeini introduced Islamic rule based on the Shia traditions of the country, which had remained strong under the influence of the *ulama*. Yet, in a departure from traditional

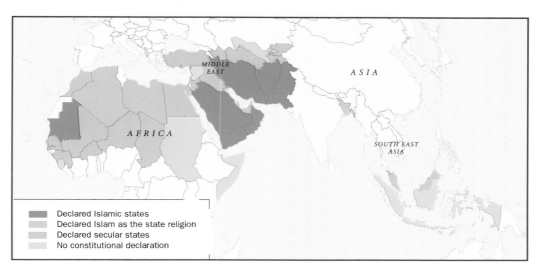

Declared Islamic states
Declared Islam as the state religion
Declared secular states
No constitutional declaration

The traditionally Muslim countries of the world and their relationship with Islam.

Shia doctrine, Khomeini declared that he alone would have absolute political and religious authority in Iran. A strict Islamic code of dress and behaviour was enforced: women had to wear the veil, alcohol and Western music were banned, and Islamic punishments were introduced. Khomeini imprisoned or killed all who opposed him.

Worldwide problems Muslims have been affected by conflict in non-Muslim countries too. In the 1990s and early 2000s, Muslims around the world grew concerned about the suffering of people of their faith, for example the massacre of Muslims during the 1992–1995 war in Bosnia; the struggle in mainly

AFGHANISTAN

In 1979, the Soviet Union invaded the Muslim country Afghanistan in support of an unpopular Communist government that had taken power there. Muslim fighters, known as *mujahidin*, launched a jihad against the government and the Soviet forces. The mujahidin forced the Soviet troops out of Afghanistan in 1989. After several years of civil war, in 1996, an extreme Islamist group called the Taliban took over the country. Under the Taliban, girls were not permitted to go to school and women were forbidden to go out to work. Harsh punishments were imposed for crime, including the amputation of a hand for theft. All forms of music and sport were banned, as was television.

Muslim Chechnya for independence from Russia; and the failure of the Palestinians to achieve an independent state. The US-led war against Iraq in 2003 and subsequent occupation of the country further inflamed Muslim feelings.

Ayatollah Khomeini greets a crowd in Qom, Iran, in December 1979. In that same month, the people voted to create an Islamic Republic.

Many people tried to help their fellow Muslims, for instance by raising awareness of the issues and supporting Islamic charities working in war-torn regions. A tiny minority of Muslims turned to extreme methods. A radical Islamist movement called al-Qaeda arose in the 1990s in response to the US-led Gulf War against Iraq of 1991. The movement's spiritual leader was Osama bin Laden. Those who identified with al-Qaeda resented Western intervention in Muslim countries and were prepared to fight Western interests through acts of terrorism. The most deadly terrorist attacks were the those that took place on 11 September 2001 in New York and Washington, in the USA, in which around 3,000 people were killed. Other atrocities have taken place, including the killing of 202 people in Bali, Indonesia, in 2002 and mass-casualty bombings in India, Russia, Saudi Arabia, Morocco, Turkey, Egypt, Spain, France and the UK.

A new extremism In 2014, a Sunni Islamist movement calling itself the Islamic State (IS) exploited political instability in Iraq and the chaos of civil war in Syria to seize large areas of both countries and declare a new Islamic State – a modern caliphate. IS's brutal tactics, including mass killings, abductions and videotaped beheadings of soldiers and journalists, sparked outrage across the world. A US-led international coalition began launching attacks on IS.

Yet IS continued to attract a small minority of radicalized young Muslims to its cause, many of whom travelled from Europe to join its fighters. Militant Islamist groups in Egypt, Libya, Tunisia and Pakistan declared allegiance to IS. And in northern Nigeria, an Islamist group called Boko Haram began seizing territory in 2014 with the aim of creating an Islamic state of its own. Its leader Abubakar Shekau declared a caliphate, pledging allegiance to IS. A military coalition of West African states formed to fight Boko Haram, and by March 2015 the Islamist group had lost all the towns under its control.

This map shows the distribution of Muslims in the world today.

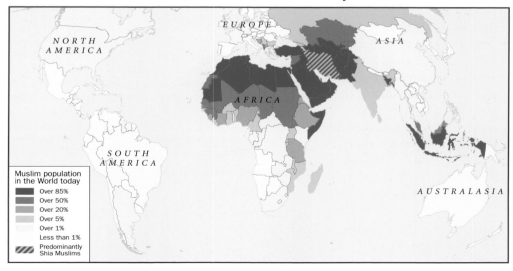

THE ARAB SPRING

Islamist movements were largely held in check by repressive regimes until 2011 when a wave of uprisings, known as the Arab Spring, erupted across the Arab world. In the countries that managed to overthrow their leaders – Tunisia, Egypt and Libya – Islamist groups were able to start exerting real political power. In surveys, people seemed supportive of parties with conservative Islamic values, though did not necessarily wish to live under a theocracy or caliphate. By 2012 more than 50 Islamist parties or movements had mobilized millions of supporters to fight elections in Arab countries. Most of these parties renounced terrorism – with the exceptions of Lebanon's Hezbollah and the Palestinian group Hamas. In Egypt, Tunisia and Morocco, the Islamists formed governments. Morocco's Justice and Development Party modelled itself on the moderate Turkish Islamist party of the same name, and it prospered. But in the case of Egypt's Freedom and Justice Party (an offshoot of the Muslim Brotherhood) and Tunisia's Ennahda, their decades-long experience as protest movements did not prepare them for the realities of government. The FJP quickly alienated moderate, secular opinion, Ennahda failed to improve the economy, and by 2014 both had fallen from power.

Islam today Because of the minority of Muslims who commit acts of terrorism, there is a growing mistrust of Muslims in general in many Western countries. Non-Muslims may see the Islamic faith as intolerant and violent. However, the majority of Muslims condemn terrorism and seek a peaceful resolution to conflict. Islam has had a significant influence over the history of the past 1,400 years. Beginning with one man in the seventh-century Arabian desert, it is now a thriving religion with 1.3 billion followers living in over 200 countries. Islam will clearly remain a religion of major significance in the 21st century.

Egyptians protest against President Morsi in Sidi Gaber, Alexandria on 30 June, 2013.

CHAPTER 4
HINDUISM

HINDUISM is perhaps the oldest living religion in the world today. It is difficult to say exactly how it started. Unlike most other faiths, it has no single founder, no one scripture, and no commonly agreed set of teachings. Throughout its long history there have been many leaders teaching different philosophies and writing thousands of holy books. Hinduism, therefore, is often called 'a family of religions', or 'a way of life'. Its roots are in ancient India, going back more than 4,000 years. Today, however, large numbers of Hindus live outside India. Many are not even of Indian descent but have adopted the teachings and practice of Hinduism. So, even though Hinduism is connected to India, it also has many followers in other parts of the world.

Ancient Indian wisdom Many Hindu followers say that their tradition is derived from sacred texts called the Vedas. *Veda*, is an ancient Sanskrit word meaning 'knowledge'. Hinduism does not limit its idea of truth to a single faith or creed but encourages flexibility of thought. To Hindus, being a good person is more important than what you believe. Despite this, most Hindus share certain key beliefs, such as the existence of the eternal soul, which is reincarnated continuously.

These ancient teachings were initially passed on by word of mouth. According to tradition, they were first written down about 5,000 years ago, although many scholars believe the texts to be much younger, dating the first book, the *Rig Veda*, to around 1000 BCE.

The eternal religion The term *Hinduism* is not found in the Vedas. Instead, they discuss *dharma*, which is often translated as 'religious duty'. More precisely, it means 'duties that sustain us according to who we are'. There are two main types of dharma:

1.   *Sanatana dharma*: actions based on the eternal relationship between the *atman* (soul) and God.
2.   *Varnashrama dharma*: duties according to the specific body we have, determined according to four *varnas* (social classes) and four *ashramas* (stages of life).

Many Hindus prefer to call their tradition *Sanatana dharma* – the eternal religion.

The creation of the material world

Hindu books, such as the *Rig Veda*, describe an eternal world made of Brahman (spirit). They also discuss the repeated creation and destruction of this material world. Even after the present universe is destroyed, it is recreated as part of an everlasting cycle.

According to the Vedas, the Earth is only one of many planets, which exist in different locations and dimensions. Although India is just one place on planet Earth, Hindus consider it special, a sacred land where many saints and avatars (incarnations of God) have lived.

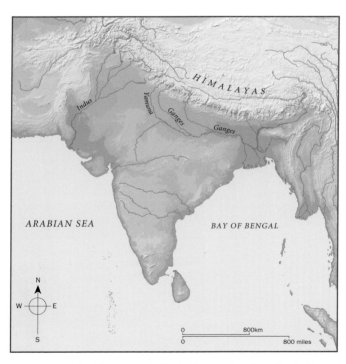

The geographical features of the Indian peninsula – the Indian subcontinent. Bounded to the north by the Himalayas, to the west by the Arabian Sea and to the east by the Bay of Bengal, India is most vulnerable to attack through its north-west frontier.

Traditional accounts of history

Hinduism's early history is complex and there are many different accounts of it. There are three main reasons for this. Firstly, Hinduism is not a single religion, but includes many distinct branches. Secondly, there are differences of opinion between Hindus and Western researchers. Thirdly, Hinduism has no definitive starting point. It is at least 4,000 or 5,000 years old, but may be much older. To study Hinduism thoroughly, it is important to understand its concept of time and its long history.

Hindus believe that since the creation of this universe, time has moved through cycles of four ages – golden, silver, copper and iron – which repeat continuously like the four seasons. During the golden age, people were virtuous and religious, but these good qualities diminished through the silver and copper ages until the present materialistic age, called the *Kali Yuga*, the age of iron; meaning literally 'the age of quarrel'.

There are two great Hindu epic poems that arguably shed some light on Indian history, though some people consider them fictional rather than historical. The first, the *Ramayana*, tells the famous story of Rama and Sita, which may have taken place in the age of silver. The second is the *Mahabharata*, meaning 'the history of greater India'.

PRAYER FROM THE RIG VEDA

Om. Oh Lord, the past, present and future universes are exhibitions of your powers, but You are greater still. The material creation is only one quarter of the entire cosmos. The eternal spiritual sky is much larger, making up the remaining three-quarters.

Rig Veda, Chapter 10, Hymn 190

The spiritual and material worlds. Hindus believe that the spiritual realm is eternal. For them, even this material world goes on forever, in an endless cycle of creation, destruction and re-creation.

Mahabharata This epic poem tells the story of five princes called the Pandavas at the very end of the last (copper) age. They were sons of King Pandu and descendants of King Bharat, after whom India is named. (India's traditional name, 'Bharatavarsha', means 'the land of Bharat', often shortened to 'Bharata'.) The Pandavas' cousins, known as the Kauravas, tried to usurp the throne of the vast Indian Empire. After much intrigue, and requests for a peaceful settlement, the Kauravas refused to give up any of the land they had occupied illegally. To support the Pandavas, or to oppose them, kings from all over the known world prepared for battle on the plains of Kurukshetra, north of present-day New Delhi.

Just prior to the great battle, Lord Krishna – one of the most important Hindu deities – recited the *Bhagavad Gita* (now a key Hindu text) to Arjuna, one of the five Pandavas. Arjuna, though a great warrior, was depressed at the prospect of fighting against his own cousins. Krishna explained all the important Vedic concepts, starting with the idea that the true self (atman) is not the body. Upon hearing the words of the *Bhagavad Gita*, Arjuna regained his composure and resolved to fight. He and his brothers emerged victorious, securing the throne of the Indian Empire. Thirty-six years later, Krishna departed the world, marking the start of the present age.

The Aryan invasion theory

When Europeans first arrived in India, they knew little of the origins of Hinduism. Finding few historical records, they studied religious accounts of history, but considered them mythological and therefore unreliable. They noted, however, that the Hindu scriptures talked of 'Aryans'. The Sanskrit word *Aryan* literally means 'noble people', but academics suggested that it referred to a distinct race of people.

Krishna and Arjuna blow their conch shells prior to the great Battle of Kurukshetra. Thirty-six years later, Krishna's departure from the world marked the start of the current age, the Kali Yuga (age of iron).

Ruins at Mohenjo-daro in present-day Pakistan. This site, and the one at Harappa, were excavated in the 1920s.

The German-born scholar and Sanskrit philologist Max Müller suggested that the Aryans had come from outside India, from the West, bringing with them the ancient Sanskrit language and the beginnings of Hinduism as we know it today.

However, little was known of the Aryan people. Then, in the 1920s, archaeologists unearthed the remains of two walled cites, Mohenjo-daro and Harappa (both in present-day Pakistan), in the valley of the River Indus. There was evidence of detailed town planning, with orderly streets and sophisticated drainage systems. Most of the houses in Mohenjo-daro had small bathrooms and there is evidence of a large tank or bath surrounded by a veranda. Both towns had a citadel where it seems religious ceremonies were carried out.

The inhabitants had even developed what appears to be a form of writing, depicted on various seals found throughout the sites. One seal portrays a figure that resembles Lord Shiva, now an

KEY HINDU IDEAS FOUND IN THE BHAGAVAD GITA

atman – the real, eternal self, which is neither the mind nor the body.

Brahman – eternal spirit, different from temporary matter (*prakriti*).

samsara – the cycle of repeated birth and death through reincarnation.

karma – the law of action and reaction: good actions bring a good next life, and vice-versa.

God – perceived in three places: everywhere (as the world soul); in the heart (in humans, as conscience); and beyond the world (as the Supreme Being).

important Hindu deity. To date, experts have been unable to decipher the script.

This Indus Valley civilization reached its height between 2600 and 1900 BCE, predating the Aryan invasion, which historians estimate started in approximately 1800 BCE. The discovery therefore challenged the theory that the Aryans were the most advanced race of their time.

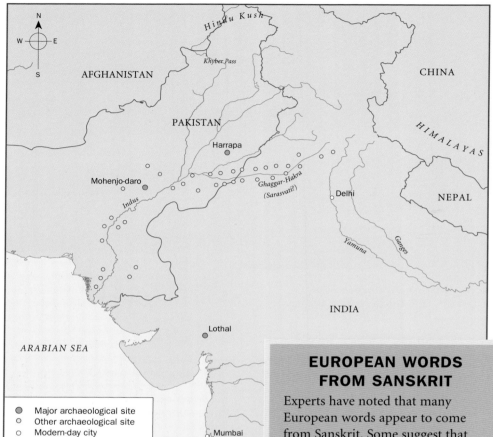

This map shows excavation sites in the Indus and Sarasvati valleys. The course of the legendary River Sarasvati is uncertain, but it may correspond to the Ghaggar-Hakra River (as shown here).

Map labels: AFGHANISTAN, CHINA, Khyber Pass, Hindu Kush, PAKISTAN, HIMALAYAS, Harrapa, Mohenjo-daro, Indus, Ghaggar-Hakra (Sarasvati?), Delhi, NEPAL, Yamuna, Ganges, INDIA, Lothal, ARABIAN SEA, Mumbai

Legend:
- Major archaeological site
- Other archaeological site
- Modern-day city

Revised theories Rather than abandoning the original invasion theory, scholars revised it. They proposed that the light-skinned Aryan invaders had conquered and destroyed the cities of the much older Indus Valley civilization. Subsequently, Aryan beliefs and practices blended with those of the local peoples, including the darker-skinned Dravidians from the south, giving rise to what we now call Hinduism. More recent archaeological finds indicate that the Indus Valley civilization was more widespread than had been first imagined. They also support the possibility that the legendary River Sarasvati (now dried up) really existed. Therefore, if the river was not a myth, then perhaps the traditional Hindu accounts of history should be taken more seriously. Hindu texts make no mention of an Aryan invasion. Although scholars are now studying the possibility that Hinduism developed within India and not outside it, it is unlikely that anyone will establish its origins conclusively.

Vedic literature Hindu teachings were first passed down by word of mouth, and later written down. Tradition states that a sage called Vyasa recorded the teachings on palm leaves about 5,000 years ago. Scholars claim that the first books, the four Vedas, were composed more recently, around 1000 BCE. The period from about 1500 to 500 BCE is known as 'the Vedic age'. The Vedas included hymns and chants for use in rituals, as well as sections on philosophy. The four Vedas are:

- the *Rig Veda* – hymns to various deities
- the *Yajur Veda* – a handbook for priests to use during yajna (sacrifices)
- the *Sama Veda* – chants and melodies
- the *Artharva Veda* – additional hymns and mantras

A havan, attended largely by members of the royal and priestly varnas (social classes).

As well as the four Vedas, Vedic literature also consists of hundreds of later texts based upon them. These writings fall into one of two broad categories: the *shruti* ('that which is heard' – the most important texts of Hinduism, regarded as authorless) and the *smriti* ('that which is remembered' – texts attributed to an author).

The Vedic age The main deities during the Vedic age were connected to nature, perhaps because the Vedas emphasized the need to live in harmony with the rhythms of nature, called *rita*. The chief deity was Indra, the rain god, also called 'the king of heaven'. Agni was also important, as he presided over the sacred fire into which all offerings were made.

THE MAIN VEDIC TEXTS

shruti – 'that which is heard'
- The Vedas (prayers and philosophy)
- The *Upanishads* (philosophy)

smriti – 'that which is remembered'
- The *Vedanta Sutra* (aphorisms)
- The *Puranas* (stories and histories)
- The epics: (1) The *Ramayana*
             (2) The *Mahabharata*
- The *Bhagavad Gita* (philosophy)
- The *Dharma Shastra* (moral codes)

During the Vedic age, priests performed elaborate *yajnas*. The most popular yajna was the *havan* (sacred fire ceremony), in which priests tossed grains into the flames as an offering to various deities. The havan was accompanied by the chanting of mantras. A mantra is a string of sacred syllables. For a sacrifice to be successful, it was essential that the mantras were pronounced correctly.

Gradually, the importance of ritual diminished as priority was given to philosophical thought. Ideas were gleaned from specific sections of the Vedas, called the *Upanishads*, and were later summarized in an anthology of aphorisms, now known as the *Vedanta Sutra*, or the *Brahma Sutra*.

THE MURTI

The *murti* (sacred statue) remains an essential feature of Hindu worship. The temple *murtis* are treated with respect, as if they are great kings and queens. Each day, the priests bathe and dress the deities, garland them with flowers and offer vegetarian food and other items of worship. Hindu families often worship small *murtis* at their home shrines. Sacred texts explain that God – invisible to most of us – appears through the *murti* to accept the worshipper's devotion. However, for God to be present, these practices must be performed according to strict rules, requiring cleanliness, punctuality and devotion.

Hindu kingdoms The scholars who taught from these sacred books belonged to the priestly varna (class) and were dedicated to spiritual life. They were not paid, but were instead dependent upon the financial support of pious Hindu kings, who were members of the warrior varna. Since ancient times, the warrior and priestly varnas had cooperated to

Temple murtis *of Sita and Rama, accompanied by Rama's brother Lakshmana (left) and the monkey warrior Hanuman (kneeling). Between 500* BCE *and 500* CE, *temple* puja *took over from* yajna *(sacrifice) as the main method of worship.*

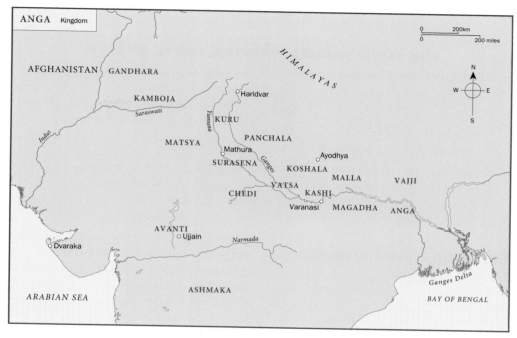

The 16 ancient Hindu kingdoms stretched from Afghanistan in the west to the Ganges delta in the east. Most were situated either around the Doab, the fertile area between the Ganges and the Yamuna, or further down the Ganges after the joining of the two rivers at Prayag.

protect and educate the general citizens. By 600 BCE, 16 Hindu kingdoms stretched across the Indian plains, from modern-day Afghanistan to beyond the Ganges delta.

The Mauryan Empire (c. 321–184 BCE)

Towards the end of the Vedic period, a leader named Chandragupta Maurya ascended the throne of the kingdom of Magadha. He extended his territory to establish the Mauryan Empire, the most powerful of ancient India. During the Mauryan era, many important texts were compiled. Chandragupta's close advisor, Chanakya, compiled the *Artha Shastra*, dealing with war, economics and political philosophy, as well as the *Niti Shastra*, a collection of proverbs still read widely today.

Earlier, oral texts were written down around this time, including the *Manu Smriti* (Laws of Mankind), which formed a part of the Vedic canon called the *Dharma Shastra* (Moral Codes). The two Hindu epics were also written down – the *Ramayana* by Valmiki and the *Mahabharata* by Vyasa. These works explored the ideal of performing one's dharma (religious duty), and especially the key role played by chivalrous kings and their learned advisers, the *Brahmins* (priests).

Puja

From 500 BCE, the complex rituals and sacrifices of Hinduism, such as the havan, were gradually superseded by *puja*, the worship of *murtis* (sacred statues). At the same time, the focus of worship moved from Indra and the other early Vedic gods, to three main deities: Vishnu, Shiva and Shakti (the goddess, also called Devi). Later, during the Gupta era, many magnificent temples were dedicated to these principal deities.

THE FOUR VARNAS AND THE CASTE SYSTEM

The *Rig Veda* describes four *varnas* (social classes):

- **Brahmins** – priests and intellectuals
- **Kshatriyas** – army, police and administrators
- **Vaishyas** – traders and business community
- **Sudras** – workers and labourers

Originally, a person was assigned to a varna according to their preference for a particular type of work. Later, the system became hereditary, and many sub-divisions (*jati*) were added. Today it is called the caste system.

The Gupta Empire (320–550 CE)

The Mauryan Empire eventually collapsed. Following a period of instability, the Gupta Empire arose and for two centuries ruled all land north of the Vindhya Range. Though not as vast as the Mauryan, the Gupta Empire left a deep cultural impression on India, and the Gupta era is now considered a golden age of Hinduism, marked by considerable achievement in religious art, music, literature, philosophy and architecture. With the increasing popularity of puja, many impressive temples were constructed. Hindu ideas extended deep into South-East Asia, reaching countries such as Cambodia, where the temples in Angkor Wat were dedicated to Vishnu and Shiva.

With the rise of temple worship, three main traditions emerged, focusing their respective worship on Vishnu, Shiva and Shakti. At the same time, the idea of the Trimurti (three main deities) developed: Brahma was considered responsible for creation, Vishnu became 'the sustainer and protector', and the role of destroyer was given to Shiva (previously known as Rudra). Shiva's wife is Shakti, also called

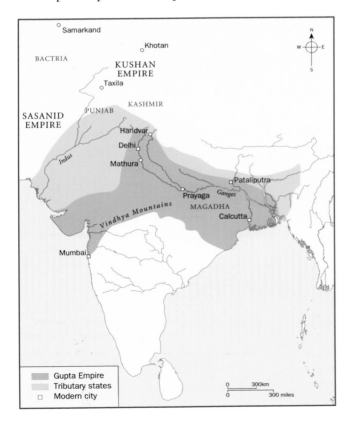

Gupta Empire
Tributary states
Modern city

The Gupta Empire under King Chandragupta II, in around 400 CE.

Devi, Durga or Parvati. Shaktas (followers of Shakti) also venerate the wives of the two other deities of the Trimurti – Lakshmi (wife of Vishnu and goddess of fortune) and Sarasvati (wife of Brahma and goddess of learning).

The Puranas During the Gupta era, the *Puranas*, or 'ancient stories', were written down. There were 18 principal tales dedicated to Brahma, Vishnu and Shiva, but with some references to Shakti. The most famous are those that describe the activities of Krishna, a form of Vishnu. Krishna is celebrated for his mischievous activities as a child and youth in the village of Vrindavana, and especially for stealing butter and feeding it to the monkeys. Another popular tale, the *Devi Bhagavata Purana*, tells the story of the goddess Durga. She slayed a demon who took the form of a buffalo. Durga easily defeated him, surpassing the might of all the gods combined.

The Chola Empire (850–1279)

The Gupta Empire collapsed around 550 CE. Power in India gradually shifted southwards. The Chola dynasty, which had been in existence since the first century CE, established an empire in the ninth century. They were devotees of Shiva, but also supported Vaishnavism and Shaktism. The Cholas built many impressive temples, particularly in Thanjavur and in their capital, Chidambaram. These temples featured large *gopurams*, towering gateways decorated with ornate carvings of deities. Shiva remained the most popular god, particularly in his form as Nataraja, the 'king of dancers'.

THE GREAT TRADITIONS

The three main traditions that emerged during the Gupta period were:

- **Vaishnavas** – who worship Vishnu
- **Shaivas** – who worship Shiva
- **Shaktas** – who worship Shakti (Devi)

Later, around the ninth century CE, another tradition developed, known as Smarta. Its followers, called Smartas, worship five deities: Vishnu, Shiva, Devi, Surya (the sun god) and Ganesh (a deity with an elephant's head). Brahma, though one of the Trimurti, is little worshipped today, except in one town in India (Pushkar in Rajasthan) and in some parts of South-East Asia.

Indian dancers perform a dance retelling the story of Durga, a fierce form of the goddess Shakti. Durga has ten arms, wielding various weapons.

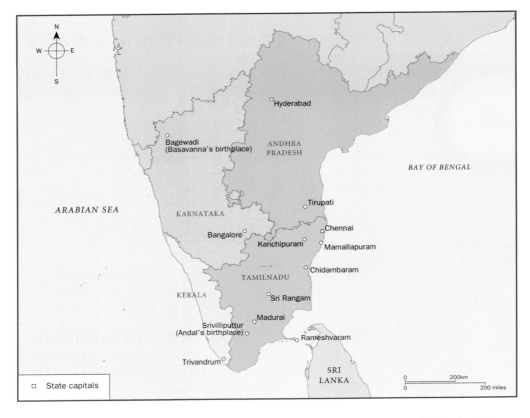

Hinduism in South-East Asia

Hinduism may have reached places such as Cambodia as early as the first century CE. With the aid of its fleet, the Chola Empire colonized countries further to the south and south-east, including the Maldives, Sri Lanka and the lands of the largely Buddhist Srivijaya Empire in Indonesia, which included Malaya, Java and Sumatra. Chola armies exacted tribute from rulers on the Indochinese Peninsula, especially from Siam (Thailand) and the Khmer kingdom of Cambodia.

Around this time, Hinduism reached the island of Bali, where it is still the main religion. Throughout South-East Asia, Hindu beliefs and practices intertwined with Buddhist and local traditions. This mixed culture still exists in many parts of Indochina and Indonesia, as is evident in the continuing use of long Sanskrit names.

The four states in southern India, showing locations connected to the poet-saints.

The poet-saints of South India

Between the sixth and tenth centuries, a group of spiritual figures known as poet-saints, who lived in southern India, helped to move Hinduism away from the strict, Brahmin-controlled rituals of the Vedic times. The poet-saints' focus on a personal God laid the foundations for modern Hinduism. They wrote in the Tamil tongue, establishing its importance as a sacred language, much like Sanskrit in the north.

Among the poet-saints were the 63 Nayanars. Worshippers of Shiva and largely unconcerned with philosophical study, they dedicated themselves to practical service, such as cleaning the temple premises, lighting the lamps,

A statue of
Nataraja from
South India

establish the important tradition now called Shaiva Siddhanta.

The Vaishnavas (Vishnu-worshipping) equivalents of the Nayanars were the 12 Alvars. Most famous was the female saint Andal, who as a young girl resolved to accept only Krishna as her husband. She was ritually married to the image of Krishna. According to legend, as the ceremony concluded, she miraculously disappeared into the *murti*. Andal's life and poetry are still celebrated during a festival that falls in December or January. The poems of the 12 Alvars were compiled into the 4,000 verses of the *Divya Prabhandham*, which remains a core text in South India. It sings the praises of Vishnu in his form as the four-handed Narayan. It is still recited daily in the famous Srirangam Temple on the banks of the River Kaveri (one of India's seven sacred rivers).

stringing flower garlands, feeding the devotees and performing other humble tasks around the temple. They regarded serving Lord Shiva's devotees to be paramount, even higher than the worship of Shiva himself. The Nayanars helped

THE ROLE OF THE TEMPLE

Within Hinduism, the temple (*mandir*) is considered the home of God, or of the specific deity whose image stands in the central shrine. The main act of worship (*arti*), is performed up to six or seven times each day. During this welcoming ceremony, the priest offers the deities pleasing items such as incense, water, flowers and a lamp. There are two main traditional styles of temple architecture: northern and southern. Northern temples feature a central shrine, a main spire (and often other smaller spires) and rounded arches. Southern temples are often situated within large complexes and are surrounded by several concentric walls. The central shrine is reached by entering towering gopurams (gateways), each profusely decorated with carvings of gods and goddesses.

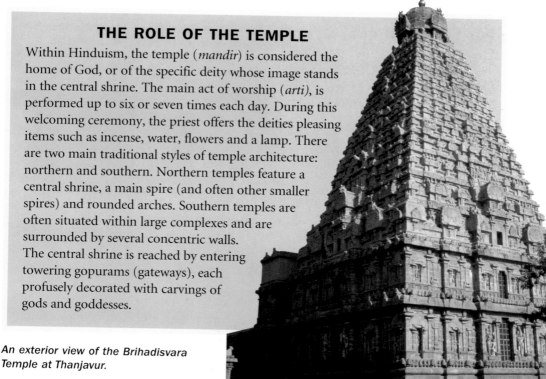

An exterior view of the Brihadisvara
Temple at Thanjavur.

FOUR GOALS AND FOUR PATHS

Hindu teachings list four goals for human life:

- *dharma* – performing religious duties.
- *artha* – developing wealth and prosperity.
- *kama* – enjoying the pleasures of the senses in an ethical way.
- *moksha* – gaining liberation from birth and death.

There are four *margs* (paths) towards *moksha*, also called *yogas*, or 'ways of linking' to God. They are:

- *karma-yoga* – the path of selfless work.
- *jnana-yoga* – the path of philosophy and wisdom.
- *astanga-yoga* – the path of exercises and meditation.
- *bhakti-yoga* – the path of devotional service. This is the most popular yoga today, though it is often mixed with practices from the three other yogas.

Bhakti movements The poet-saints came from all walks of life and cared little for the Hindu social structure, which by then had evolved into the hereditary caste system. By accepting disciples from all social classes, the poet-saints challenged the authority of the Brahmins (priests).

The poet-saints gave rise to popular *bhakti* movements (movements of religious devotion) that later swept north to embrace all of India. One of the first was founded in the 12th century by a scholar named Basavanna. Members of the movement were called Lingayats, after the small *lingam* they always carried. The sacred lingam is a cylindrical black stone believed to represent Lord Shiva. The Lingayats believed in one God and rejected the Vedas for their polytheism. Lingayats preached the equality of all beings, and – unusually for the time – accepted women as gurus.

Devotional activities inside a temple in India. The women are praying and making offerings to a large lingam, *the symbol of Shiva, while a priest reads from holy scripture.*

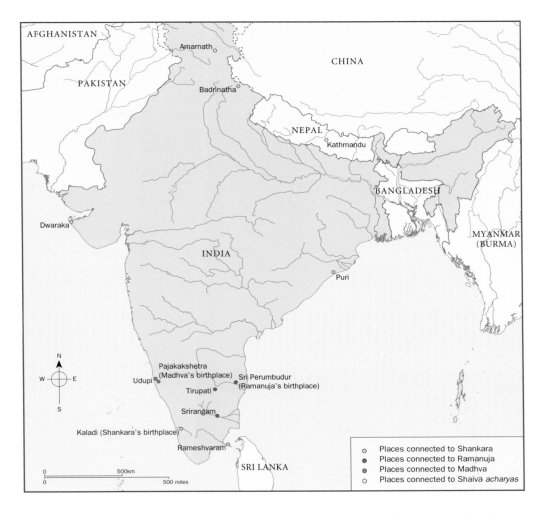

The map shows labeled locations including:

AFGHANISTAN, PAKISTAN, CHINA, NEPAL, Kathmandu, BANGLADESH, MYANMAR (BURMA), INDIA, SRI LANKA

Amarnath, Badrinatha, Dwaraka, Puri, Pajakakshetra (Madhva's birthplace), Udupi, Sri Perumbudur (Ramanuja's birthplace), Tirupati, Srirangam, Kaladi (Shankara's birthplace), Rameshvaram

N / W — E / S compass

0 500km
0 500 miles

○ Places connected to Shankara
● Places connected to Ramanuja
● Places connected to Madhva
○ Places connected to Shaiva *acharyas*

Scholars and philosophers

Around the time of the poet-saints, several key thinkers, or *acharyas*, laid the foundations for modern Hindu thought. Each acharya started his own branch of philosophy. To spread their ideas, they each established a sampradaya, an unbroken succession of teachers and students (who in turn become teachers). The acharyas reinforced the importance of the relationship between the guru and the disciple. For them, knowledge was not merely about gathering information, but was also about developing character and understanding through moral conduct and discipline.

The cities and holy sites connected to the major Hindu philosophers and scholars.

Vedanta philosophy

The acharyas taught different versions of Vedanta philosophy. *Vedanta* means 'the conclusion of the Vedas', and is one of the six *darshans* ('orthodox' schools) in Hinduism. The darshans are not entirely distinct schools of thought, but represent different ways of viewing the same truth. Vedanta developed two main ideas about God: first, that he is impersonal, the ever-present world soul; and second, that God is ultimately a person, living beyond this material world. Many traditions combine these two views.

Acharyas Adi Shankara (c. 780–812) was born in what is today the southern state of Kerala. According to legend, he renounced the world at the age of eight to become a *sannyasi* (wandering monk). He later accepted initiation from a spiritual teacher, who asked him to write commentaries on Vedanta philosophy. At this time, Hinduism was losing some of its appeal because of the widespread influence of Buddhism and Jainism. Hindus had accepted Buddha as an avatar (incarnation) of Vishnu. Nonetheless, many Hindus considered Buddhists and Jains unorthodox for their rejection of the Vedic texts.

Shankara travelled throughout India, reestablishing the authority of the Vedic literature and defeating opposing arguments. He started the *Advaita* school of Vedanta, teaching that the soul and God are identical. He founded a fourth strand of Hinduism called the *Smarta* school (see page 117), distinct from the already existing Vaishnava, Shaiva and Shakta traditions. Shankara also established monasteries in locations in the north, east, south and west of India – the four cardinal directions.

Ramanuja (1017–1137) was the most important acharya among the Sri Vaishnava sampradaya of South India. According to Ramanuja, God not only exists everywhere as a formless energy (as Shankara taught), but is also a person with a spiritual body. Salvation is obtained largely through grace, by which the soul (atman) enters Vishnu's abode to live forever in a spiritual form. Today, Tirupati and Srirangam in South India remain the main centres of Sri Vaishnavism.

Another acharya, Madhva (1238–1317), stressed the personal form of God (as Krishna) and the eternal distinction between God and the atman. The headquarters of the Madhva tradition are in Udupi in the state of Karnataka.

Ramanuja and Madhva were both Vaishnavas. There were also several Shaiva (Shiva-worshipping) acharyas, including Abhinavagupta, Srikantha and Bhojadeva, who taught their own philosophies.

A traditional painting of Adi Shankara.

Muslim-dominated India

By the 11th century, while Hindu kingdoms flourished in the south, religious life was threatened in the north. The relatively new religion of Islam had first reached India through traders plying the Arabian Sea in the seventh century. In the eighth century, Iraqi Arabs occupied the north-western state of Sindh. Muslims from Turkey and Central Asia gradually superseded Persia (Iran) as the major power to the west of India.

In 1192, the Muslim ruler Muhammad of Ghor defeated the Hindu king Prithviraj and overran the city of Delhi. This marked the beginning of over five centuries of Muslim rule in India. It was to have a significant effect on the way Hinduism developed. Islam was sometimes hostile towards Hinduism, especially the practice of image worship. The ancient tradition of

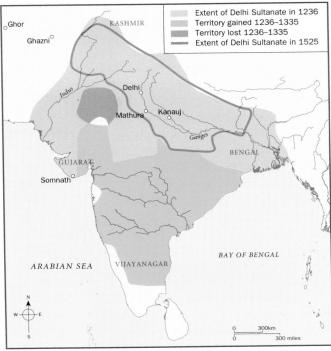

The rise and decline of the Delhi Sultanate from 1236 to 1525, the year before the Mughal invasion led by Babur.

Sanatana dharma (Hinduism), known for its inclusivity and tolerance, was forced to redefine itself. The term *Hindu*, referring to the people living on the far side of the River Indus, had first been coined by the Persians in the seventh century. By the 1400s, it had also been adopted by those who practised the faith, to distinguish themselves from members of other religions.

The courtyard of the Quwwat-ul-Islam mosque, in the Mehrauli district of New Delhi. An outstanding monument from the era of Muslim rule in India; work on the mosque began in 1193 CE.

The Hindu social system

By the time the Muslims arrived, the ancient Indian system of four varnas had become hereditary (the modern caste system). Birth into a high family usually guaranteed a prestigious job, even for the unqualified. Those born into the lower castes were forced into menial work, despite any talent they may have had for other professions. Muslim rule created a governing elite, reinforcing class differences and bolstering the caste system. Under many Muslim rulers, Hindus were required to pay special taxes. They were also sometimes forcibly converted to Islam. About a quarter of Hindus converted, mainly in the north-west and in Bengal.

The Mughal Empire

In 1398, Delhi was destroyed by Timur, a Muslim conqueror who claimed descent from the Mongol emperor, Genghis Khan. The Delhi Sultanate (the Muslim dynasty ruling India) never fully recovered, and eventually, in 1526, Delhi fell to Babur, a Muslim descendent of Timur from Central Asia. Babur subsequently established the Mughal dynasty, which ruled much of India for the following three centuries.

One of the Mughal Empire's greatest rulers was Akbar, Babur's grandson (ruled

STORIES OF BIRBAL

Birbal, a Hindu, was one of the 'nine jewels' in Akbar's court. As Akbar's prime minister, he was known for his extraordinary wit. There are many tales about Birbal and how he avoided the intrigues of court rivals. These stories, still popular with Hindus, often feature in comics and on television. They are part of the tradition of passing down wisdom through the medium of story.

Dating from the Mughal period, this painting depicts Krishna and his girlfriend, Radha. During Akbar's reign, Hindu art, music and architecture flourished, though much was later destroyed by the ruthless Aurangzeb.

The growth of the Mughal Empire from the death of Akbar in 1605 until 1700. By the end of the 17th century, European traders had established several important outposts, which threatened Mughal supremacy.

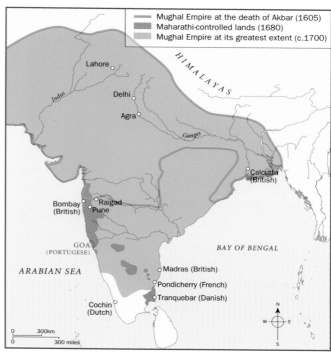

Mughal Empire at the death of Akbar (1605)
Maharathi-controlled lands (1680)
Mughal Empire at its greatest extent (c.1700)

1542–1605). Born and raised in India, Akbar displayed a positive attitude towards all religions. He celebrated Hindu festivals and began a series of religious debates to which he invited not only Muslims, but also Hindus, Sikhs and Christians. He also encouraged members of other faiths to enter his government.

Akbar was succeeded by his son, Jahangir, and then his grandson, Shah Jahan. Shah Jahan's son, Aurangzeb, was tyrannical. During his long reign (1668–1707), he discriminated against Hindus, imposing heavy taxes on them and defacing their temples and sacred images. Aurangzeb's religious policies contributed to Muslim–Hindu conflict in India, creating resentment that endures to modern times.

New Hindu kingdom

During the period of Muslim rule, the wealthy city of Vijayanagar (City of Victory) resisted the military might of both the Delhi Sultanate and the Mughals until its final collapse in 1565. This marked the end of the south as a separate political region. However, a more formidable foe of the Mughals emerged on the west coast of India, in the mountainous Maharathi kingdom. The Maharathi king Shivaji (1630–1680)

and his successors harassed Aurangzeb relentlessly, hastening the end of Mughal rule. Shivaji was a resistance fighter who exemplified the ancient Hindu ideal of the pious and chivalrous warrior. For many modern Hindus, he remains a symbol of the righteous struggle against oppression.

Bhakti sweeps India

The restraints of Mughal rule were compounded by the tight control exercised by Hindu priests. Many of these Brahmins insisted on the strict observation of the hereditary caste system, which barred Hindus of lower birth from fully participating in religious life or society. Ordinary Hindus felt marginalized. Leaders arose from among their ranks, stressing the spiritual equality of all and the personal relationship everyone could develop with God. As a result, a wave of *bhakti*, or religious devotion, swept through India.

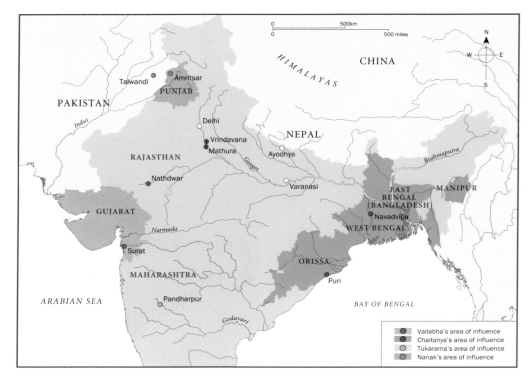

The principal states and towns on the Indian peninsula that are still influenced today by four of the prominent bhakti *saints and their respective teachings.*

Bhakti saints The leaders of this movement, called the *bhakti* saints, drew on the religious sentiments of the earlier South Indian poet-saints and also on Vedanta philosophy, especially as taught by Ramanuja and Madhva. While the poet-saints had worshipped Shiva and Vishnu, these largely northern traditions focused on Rama and Krishna, two principal avatars of Vishnu.
Important saints at the time included:

- **Chaitanya**, who founded Bengali Vaishnavism.
- **Kabir**, who taught that God is the same for everyone, whatever path they choose to tread. His followers included Muslims, Sikhs and Hindus.
- **Vallabha**, who favoured the worship of baby Krishna, a custom that is still popular with many Gujarati Hindus.

- **Surdas**, who was born blind but became an excellent musician and composed thousands of songs glorifying Krishna.
- **Tulsidas**, who wrote a popular version of the *Ramayana*, known as *Rama Carita Manas*.
- **Tukarama**, who worshipped the famous deity of Vishnu, known as Vitthala, in Pandharpur (present-day Maharashtra, near Mumbai).
- **Mirabai**, who is perhaps the most famous female saint within Hinduism.

Music, mantra and dance
Many bhakti traditions popularized the chanting of mantras, either out loud to music or softly on prayer beads. The saints also composed their own songs, poems and prayers in local languages. The Bengali saint Chaitanya was renowned for chanting and dancing in public.

He popularized the following mantra:

> *Hare Krishna, Hare Krishna,*
> *Krishna Krishna, Hare Hare,*
> *Hare Rama, Hare Rama,*
> *Rama Rama, Hare Hare.*

On the other side of India, Mirabai, a Rajasthani princess, became renowned for her devotion to Krishna, despite persecution from her family. She finally abandoned palace life to become a wandering saint. Her religious love poems are still recited today. They express intense feelings of separation from God, a mood shared by many bhakti saints.

The birth of the Sikh religion

Guru Nanak (1469–1539), the founder of the Sikh religion, was influenced by the northern bhakti tradition. He taught the importance of chanting God's holy names, the equality of all people and the importance of *seva* (service to others). Nanak's new faith was at first closely connected to Hinduism. It was only later

Chaitanya dancing: he opposed the hereditary caste system and emphasized the importance of developing love for a personal God.

that it became a separate religion. Sikhism also took on a military aspect, as its members fought against the Mughals, and later the British. (See Chapter 6.)

British Rule in India (1757–1947)

In 1498, Vasco da Gama became the first European to set foot in India, at Calicut on the west coast. Subsequently, in 1510, the Portuguese conquered Goa. The splendour and wealth of the Mughal Empire also attracted the interest of French, Dutch and British traders. In 1610, the British East India Company established a base in Surat and further posts in Madras (1639), Bombay (1668) and Calcutta (1690). The administrators of the company signed trade agreements with the Mughals and recruited local men for their own military force.

As the East India Company expanded its influence, tensions arose between the company and both local and central rulers, which led to conflict. Robert Clive's victory at the Battle of Plassey (1757) in Bengal heralded the end of the Mughal Empire. By 1769, the East India Company had almost taken complete control of European trade in India.

Indian troops fighting on the side of Robert Clive during his victory at Plassey in 1757.

In 1857, a rumour spread among Indian soldiers that their rifle bullets were greased with the fat of cows and pigs, suggesting a disregard for the beliefs of both Hindus and Muslims on the part of the British. As a consequence, the Indian troops rebelled in what became known as the Indian Mutiny, prompting the British to take full control of India in 1858.

Reform movements The early colonialists gave Hindus free rein in their religious practice. However, later on, some missionaries, scholars and government officials made a concerted effort to convert Hindus to Christianity and 'civilize' them, particularly through education. Their attempts at conversion, and the growing contact between Hinduism and the West, spawned various Hindu 'reform movements'.

One of the most influential was the Brahmo Sabha, founded in 1828 by Ram Mohan Roy, and later renamed the Brahmo Samaj. Strongly influenced by Christianity, Ram Mohan disagreed with reincarnation and opposed caste practices and image worship. Today, the Brahmo Samaj continues, but with a relatively small membership.

The Arya Samaj was founded in 1875 by Swami Dayananda, who wished to halt the Christian onslaught and return to the ancient, Vedic religion. The Arya Samaj opposed what it considered later additions to Hinduism, such as image worship, ritual bathing and pilgrimage. Today, the main form of worship of the Arya Samaj is the ancient fire ceremony.

These movements had relatively little effect on Hindu practices, and the main traditions continued to predominate. They did succeed, however, in making Hindus more aware of their own identity as a separate religion. They also gave rise to nationalist movements, which tried to rid India of foreign rule. Another effect of British rule was the emigration of Hindus to other parts of the Empire.

Migration to the Caribbean

Emigration from India had been a continuous process since precolonial times, mainly for reasons of trade. During the colonial period, emigration to the British, French and Dutch colonies was a way of finding work. By the end of the 19th century, emigrants from India numbered almost 1.6 million. In Britain's Caribbean colonies, the abolition of slavery (from 1834 onwards) resulted in a shortage of manpower. The colonial governments therefore turned to the 250 million inhabitants of India.

Right: India in 1857, at the time of the Indian Mutiny, also called the First War of Independence.

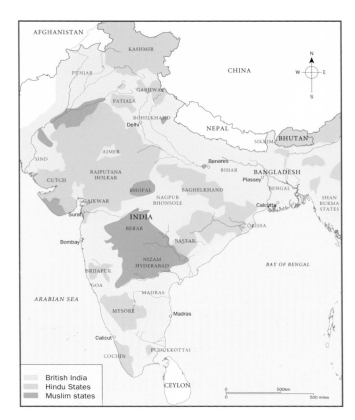

AFGHANISTAN
KASHMIR
CHINA
PUNJAB
GARHWAL
PATIALA
ROHILKHAND
Delhi
NEPAL
SIKKIM BHUTAN
AJMER
SIND
Benares
BIHAR
BANGLADESH
RAJPUTANA HOLKAR
Plassey
CUTCH
BHOPAL
BAGHELKHAND
BENGAL
SHAN BURMA STATES
GAIKWAR
NAGPUR BHONSOLE
Calcutta
Surat
INDIA
BERAR
ORISSA
Bombay
BASTAR
BAY OF BENGAL
NIZAM HYDERABAD
BRIJAPUR
GOA
MADRAS
ARABIAN SEA
MYSORE
Madras
Calicut
COCHIN
PUDUKKOTTAI
CEYLON

British India
Hindu States
Muslim states

0   500km
0   500 miles

MIGRATION AND HINDU CULTURE

Emigration affected Hindu practice, as emigrants adopted cultural habits from their host communities. Hindus abroad, especially men, began to wear Western clothes. They changed their eating habits, sometimes abandoning their traditional, often vegetarian, diets. However, in some instances Hindus living outside India became more serious about passing on their religion and culture to future generations. As with all religions, it was a struggle to maintain tradition, while at the same time adjusting to new situations.

A Hindu wedding in Trinidad and Tobago. The bride wears a traditional red and gold saree, the groom is in white silk with a gold turban.

In the 1840s, indentured labourers (workers bound by a contract) – mostly Hindi speakers from North India – were sent to work in the British Caribbean. They were promised fair wages and return tickets in exchange for agreeing to work for a set number of years. Due to poverty, the dishonest contracts of some employers, and aspirations to build a new life, very few returned to India. The first Indians to arrive became labourers for the sugar industry in Trinidad. Others sailed to French Guyana and Dutch Suriname to work on the rubber and sugar plantations.

South-East Asia and Africa

The British took formal control of the Western Malay states in 1870. Many Tamils (from Tamil Nadu in South India) subsequently moved there to become manual labourers in the tin mines or on the railways and rubber plantations. Many also moved to Singapore and Burma. Beginning in 1879, others sailed east to Fiji to work on sugar and cotton plantations. By the early 20th century, Indians constituted at least half of the population of Fiji.

Indians, including many Hindus, also migrated to the island of Mauritius, off the east coast of Africa, and to the nearby French island of Réunion. Others, largely from Gujarat, migrated to East Africa, or to South Africa to work on the railways and in the gold mines. It was in South Africa that Mohandas K. Gandhi, perhaps the most famous Hindu of contemporary times, worked as a lawyer. He was alarmed at colonial exploitation and the way Indians were treated as second-class citizens.

Indian nationalism Gandhi objected to the practice of exporting raw Indian cotton to Manchester in the UK,

HINDU VALUES

Gandhi was an avid reader of the *Bhagavad Gita*, which lists many desirable human values, such as:

- Non-violence to all (*ahimsa*).
- Respect for all living beings.
- Humility.
- Mind and sense control.
- Detachment from possessions.
- Service (*seva*) to God and to others.
- Sustainability (*sattva*).
- Cleanliness and truthfulness.

According to the *Bhagavad Gita*, without such values, individuals and societies cannot be peaceful or happy. Gandhi emphasized non-violence, based on the belief in the presence of a soul in all forms of life. For this same reason, many Hindus practise vegetarianism.

Mahatma Gandhi during the Salt March in which he personally walked the 384-kilometre route.

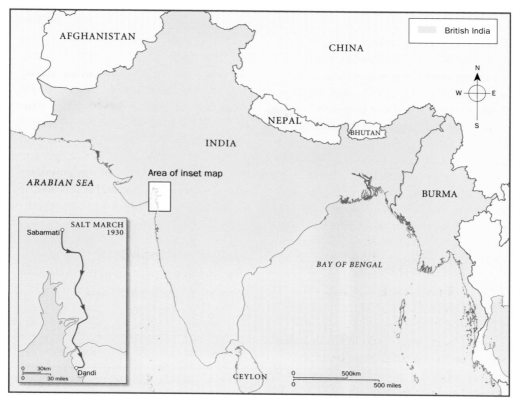

A map showing the greatest extent of India under British rule (1945). The inset map shows Gandhi's route during the salt march of 1930, a key event in the Quit India movement.

to make clothes that were then imported into India at inflated prices. He personally boycotted cloth milled in Western factories. His struggle for fair trade was part of a growing nationalist movement calling for an end to British rule and to colonial exploitation.

In 1909, leading members of the Arya Samaj founded the Hindu Mahasabha (the Great Hindu Assembly) to give Hindus a distinct political voice. The Mahasabha declared 'Hindustan' (India) to be 'the land of the Hindus' and demanded government according to Hindu law. In 1923, Vir Savarkar, leader of the Mahasabha, coined the term *Hindutva*, which translates as 'Hinduness'. It now largely refers to organizations that advocate Hindu nationalism.

These movements include the Rashtriya Swayamsevak Sangh (RSS), established in 1925 and today perhaps the most powerful Hindu organization, with around five million members worldwide.

Gandhi's movement In 1915,
Mahatma Gandhi stepped onto the political stage. He and many of his followers wore only homespun cotton, intent on undermining the British textile industry that was based in Manchester. In 1930, he organized a 384-kilometre march to the sea, where demonstrators made their own salt illegally, protesting against the British salt tax. In all these endeavours, Gandhi insisted on non-violent 'passive resistance', even in the face of aggression.

Gandhi and caste Gandhi drew much of his strength and conviction from the Hindu teachings. However, like the bhakti saints before him, he objected to the hereditary caste system. By his time, some people has been labelled as 'outcasts' or 'untouchables', indicating a status even lower than the fourth varna, the *shudras* (workers). Untouchables were allocated only the lowliest jobs, such as street cleaning or leather working. They were often banned from eating with others, entering temples or drawing water from village wells. Gandhi renamed the untouchables Harijans, 'the children of God'.

India and surrounding countries shortly after partition, including some areas of contention. More recently, ideas of 'sacred land' have been used to promote Hindu nationalism.

For practical purposes, Gandhi believed in the system of four varnas, but not in the hereditary system, which denied equal opportunity. He wanted to incorporate the Harijans within the fourth class, the *shudra varna*. Another reformer, Ramji Ambedkar, disagreed with Gandhi on the future status of untouchables and advocated instead a completely classless society. Ambedkar later converted to Buddhism and became a hero figure for the Harijans, who renamed themselves the Dalits (the oppressed). Their struggle for equal rights continues to this day.

Indian independence Gandhi led the initial negotiations for independence, which gathered pace after World War II (1939–1945). As independence neared,

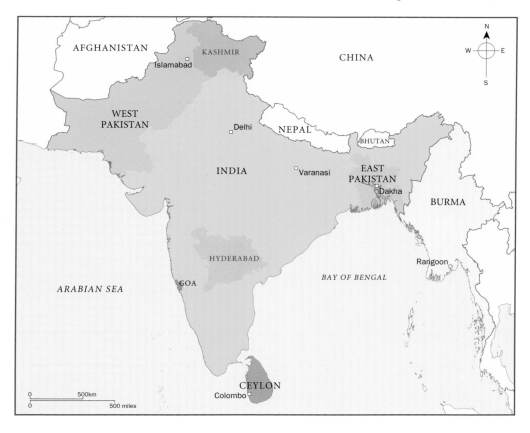

SACRED LAND

When on pilgrimage, Hindus visit what they consider sacred land – sites connected to the lives of the various saints and deities. They take darshan (audience) of the local *murtis*, accept hardships such as walking barefoot, and give to charity. A *tirtha*, meaning 'ford', is a holy town – a place where worshippers can cross over to the opposite shore (the spiritual world).

The idea of 'sacred land' has been used for political purposes. Some Hindus argue that the land of India is sacred to Hindus, and therefore India should be governed as a Hindu nation. Others claim that the Indian peninsula is special simply because it is a spiritual place and it should not belong to any one faith. The precise relationship between India and Hinduism is debatable, especially now that increasing numbers of Hindus are born and raised elsewhere, or come from non-Indian families.

undivided India was no longer possible, as Muslims were not prepared to live under a Hindu government.

When British rule ended on 15 August 1947, it was accompanied by the creation of the new state of Pakistan, comprising two Muslim-majority areas in the eastern and western parts of India. Partition was accompanied by unprecedented horrors. Around half a million people were killed as no fewer than 11 million refugees, including Hindus, Muslims and Sikhs, crossed the newly drawn borders. To this day, it remains the largest recorded human migration event. Gandhi, greatly disappointed by partition and the ensuing violence, was assassinated in 1948 by a Hindu fanatic. His former ally, Jawaharlal Nehru, became India's first prime minister.

tensions increased between Hindus and Muslims. For the minority Muslim community, the prospect of a Hindu government seemed little better than British rule. In 1946, Mohammed Jinnah, head of the Muslim League, conveyed the message that, for his community, an

Hindus bathe in the sacred waters of the River Ganges at Varanasi during a religious festival.

Kashmir After partition, India forcibly assimilated smaller territories such as Hyderabad, French India and, after some time, Portuguese Goa. Kashmir, then an independent state, chose to join India, despite having a Muslim majority. Pakistan objected, leading to the first Indo-Pakistani War (1948). A stalemate resulted in a ceasefire and, finally, the assimilation of Kashmir into India. Religious and political violence continues to this day, spoiling the prospects for a region once famed for its natural beauty and rich cultural heritage.

Nepal Although India and Pakistan were divided along religious lines, the new Indian state was secular, meaning that it was neutral in matters of religion. After partition, the only remaining Hindu

Girls dressed as Krishna (left) and his consort, Radha, at the annual Rathayatra cart festival in London. Originally celebrated in Puri, on India's east coast, the festival is now replicated in cities throughout the world.

country in the world was Nepal, north of India, on the border with southern China. Nepal declared its independence from Britain in 1923. Today, many Hindus of Nepalese origin also live in the Himalayan kingdom of Bhutan, making up 25 per cent of its population.

Migration from Uganda In 1972, Hindus and other Indians were expelled from Uganda, leaving behind considerable wealth. Holding British passports, most settled in the United Kingdom, within the inner cities. Many took on low-paid jobs or started small businesses as grocers, newsagents or clothing manufacturers. The natural centres of the new Hindu communities were the first simple temples, often converted from old buildings such as church halls. Here, Hindus practised their puja, celebrated their festivals and performed rites of passage, such as birth ceremonies, initiations and weddings. Largely poor at first, the British Hindu community gradually established itself

CELEBRATING SPECIAL OCCASIONS

Commemorating special occasions is one way that Hindus maintain and pass on their traditions to the younger generation. Hindus living outside India continue to celebrate their festivals and observe up to 16 *samskaras* (rites of passage). The most important are the birth ceremonies, the sacred-thread initiation (three strands of sacred thread are given to a boy student to wear), the wedding and the funeral. Each samskara marks a special event in the journey of life. Since ancient times, Hindus have divided human life into four distinct stages, called *ashrams*:

1. *Brahmachari ashrama* – student life
2. *Grihastha ashrama* – married life
3. *Vanaprastha ashrama* – retired life
4. *Sannyasa ashrama* – renounced life

Even today, some Hindu men still leave home to become sannyasis (monks). Some sannyasis travel abroad to train priests to conduct special ceremonies and to teach Hindus how to practise their religion outside India, within another culture.

socially and economically. By the end of 20th century, Hindus excelled in education and in the professional fields. Many magnificent purpose-built temples replaced the converted church halls, testifying to the growing prestige and influence of the Hindu community.

Migration from India During the second half of the 20th century, many Hindus emigrated directly from India. Great numbers moved to North America, especially the US, where the community now comprises almost 1.5 million. Unlike British Hindus, many of these emigrants were professionals, including doctors, engineers and IT specialists, who sought a more comfortable lifestyle. Other Indians moved to Europe, often from South India and Sri Lanka, establishing the presence of the previously under-represented South Indian Hindu traditions.

Traditional sannyasis dressed in saffron robes and carrying staffs. The Hindu emphasis on personal spirituality helped many such practices to endure, despite centuries of foreign rule and social change.

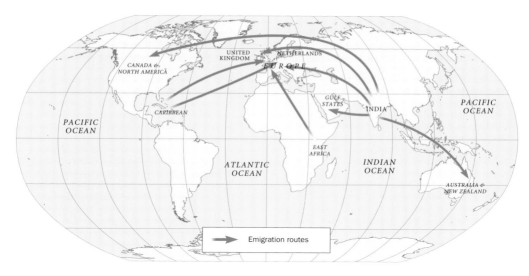

Hindu migration patterns in the latter half of the 20th century, after Indian independence.

Since 1965, many Hindus have sought work in the oil-rich Arab States around the Persian Gulf. About one million now live there, mainly in Bahrain, Kuwait, Yemen, Saudi Arabia and the United Arab Emirates. They often support families in India, where the money sent home is worth far more, due to the relatively low cost of living there.

Worldwide leaders and movements

Swami Vivekananda was a sannyasi and the first important Hindu to introduce Hinduism to the West. In 1893, he won a standing ovation at the first World's Parliament of Religions in Chicago, USA. During the post-independence emigration, many other gurus travelled west to support the growing Hindu communities. Some started their own movements, often attracting Western followers.

The hippie movement of the 1960s, with its shunning of social conventions and pursuit of a more spiritual way of life, drew much of its inspiration from India. Yoga and meditation became fashionable. The Transcendental Meditation movement, led by a guru called the Maharishi Mahesh Yogi, attracted the interest of celebrities such as the Beatles. Alternative religions, often of Eastern origin, appealed to many young people. Popular religious groups included the Divine Life Society (founded by Swami Sivananda), the Divine Light Mission (now called Elan Vital) and followers of the late and controversial guru, Rajneesh (now called Osho). One of the most noticeable was the Hare Krishna movement, whose male members shaved their heads, wore traditional saffron robes and chanted and danced on the streets of cities throughout the world.

Since the 1960s and 1970s, other Hindu groups have gained popularity. These include the Swaminarayan movement from Gujarat, which in 1995 opened an impressive, traditional stone temple near London. The Himalayan Academy is a south Indian Shaiva tradition, known for its glossy magazine entitled *Hinduism Today*. In the 2000s, a guru called Ravi Shankar and his Art of Living Foundation became influential.

Some groups and their leaders do not use the term Hinduism. They consider the term, originally given by outsiders, to be sectarian (stressing the differences between the various religious traditions). These include Sathya Sai Baba, who claims to be an incarnation of both Shiva and Shakti, and the Brahma Kumaris, whose members are mainly women.

Female gurs

Traditionally, women in Hinduism are expected to marry and serve their husbands faithfully. Despite this, there are many examples of powerful and assertive Hindu women. Some, such as Sita (from the *Ramayana*, Rama's wife), followed Hindu custom regarding dealings between men and women strictly. Others, such as Mirabai, defied convention in the name of spiritual

equality. Some traditions (though not all) have accepted women as gurus and today there are number, including Ammachi, Nirmala Devi and Mother Meera.

HINDU CULTURE

Indian and Hindu culture has made its mark throughout the world. For example, many Indian words – such as *chutney*, *pyjamas* and *bungalow* – entered the English language at the time of the British Empire. More recently, India's spiritual influence has become apparent through the widespread use of terms such as *guru*, *karma* and *avatar*. The culture has also had a big impact on Western lifestyles, with the continuing interest in yoga and meditation, complementary health treatments (such as Indian Ayurvedic remedies), home accessories (such as incense), fashion items (like nose studs), and Indian cuisine.

Members of the Hare Krishna movement chanting and dancing in Boston, North America, during the late 1960s.

Hinduism and Indian politics

India's first Prime Minister, Jawaharlal Nehru, was succeeded by Lal Shastri, and shortly afterwards by Nehru's daughter, Indira Gandhi. In 1984, during her second term of office, Sikhs lobbied for their own state in Punjab, and militants locked themselves in the most sacred Sikh temple, the Golden Temple in Amritsar. Government troops stormed the complex, infuriating the Sikh community. Indira Gandhi was subsequently assassinated by Sikh members of her personal guard. The ensuing violence further strained the previously amicable relationship between Sikhs and Hindus. Tension also continued between Hindus and Muslims. In 1992, Hindu militants destroyed the Babri mosque in Ayodhya, traditionally the site of Rama's birthplace.

The Hindutva movement, advocating Hindu nationalism, remains a strong political force in India. The conservative Hindu nationalist party, Bharatiya Janata Party (BJP), has won several elections since its formation in 1980. In 2014 it gained an absolute majority in the national parliament and formed a government under the prime ministership of Narendra Modi.

Hindu identity For Hindus in India and abroad, interaction with other cultures has raised questions about their identity. The very idea of Hinduism as a single religion, comparable to other major faiths, is relatively new. Researchers say that the word *Hinduism* was only coined in the 19th century. Hindu nationalists suggest otherwise, emphasizing that Hinduism is an Indian religion and that India should be a Hindu country. Other Hindu thinkers stress that the universal teachings of Hinduism extend well beyond India.

Indian Hindus offering special prayers for world peace in Mumbai in May 2004. More than 15,000 Hindus recited mantras while throwing unbroken grains into a sacred fire.

PRAYER FOR WORLD PEACE

May good fortune pervade the entire universe, and may all envious people be pacified. May all living beings become contented by practising bhakti-yoga, *for by accepting devotional service they will think of each other's welfare. Therefore, let us all engage in the service of the one Supreme Lord.*

Bhagavat Purana 5.18.9.

Puja ceremony on the banks of the River Ganges in Hardwar, northern India.

In attempting to relate their ancient teachings to modern life, Hindus are faced with other vital questions. Is the idea of four varnas relevant to life today? In Hindu society, should women now play an identical role to men? Can Hindus embrace modern science and medicine while remaining true to their faith?

Hinduism as a spiritual path

For many Hindus, their tradition is primarily a source of spiritual inspiration. They value worship and meditation as a means towards self-improvement and building a better world.

Many Hindus have been inspired by their religious convictions to take part in environmental projects. They believe in global karma (reaping the results of past actions), the unity of all creatures (as the atman is present in all species of life), and freedom from greed. Such principles have prompted them to help protect and conserve the planet.

Most Hindus also disagree with the proposition that any one faith is the only true faith, and stand firmly against intolerance and religious violence. They consider that God is the same for all people, despite their different belief systems.

Towards a peaceful world

Hinduism prides itself on being a peaceful religion. It teaches that without inner peace we cannot be happy. Hinduism itself faces many challenges in trying to adapt its ancient teachings to a rapidly changing world. Yet it remains a vibrant, colourful and evolving tradition. Its ancient values, based on service to others and the spiritual equality of all creatures, continue to make a positive contribution in the modern world.

CHAPTER 5
BUDDHISM

ONE OF THE world's major religions, Buddhism began in northern India some 2,500 years ago when a prince became a humble sage and taught people a new way to live. He became known as the Buddha, or the 'Enlightened One'. Since then, Buddhism has developed many different schools and spread to countries all over the world, both in its Asian homeland and beyond. In each place, it has adapted to local traditions, merged with local beliefs, and faced many changes and challenges.

The birth of the Buddha

The dates usually given for the life of Siddhartha Gautama are 563–483 BCE, although some scholars put them at 448–368 BCE, over a century later. According to tradition, he was the son of King Shuddhodana, chief of the Shakya clan who lived in north-east India, on the border with present-day Nepal. During her pregnancy, Siddhartha's mother, Queen Maya, dreamt that she was visited by a white elephant. This was a sign that the child she was carrying was destined to be a great person.

The legend of his birth states that Siddhartha was born on the night of the full moon in May in a beautiful garden in Lumbini, Nepal. Many stories illustrate that this was no ordinary birth. The gods are said to have showered the baby with flower petals, and a rumbling earthquake shook the Earth. Seven days later, Queen Maya died, and Siddhartha was brought up by his aunt in his father's palace.

A life of luxury Shortly after Siddhartha was born, a wise man called Asita came to the palace to visit the baby. Asita predicted Siddhartha's future. He told the king that his son would grow up to be either a great ruler or a great teacher, depending on what he discovered about suffering in life. Determined that Siddhartha should rule after him, the king tried to keep all knowledge of suffering from the boy. He kept Siddhartha inside his magnificent palace, sheltered from the outside world and surrounded by the finest things. As part of his education, Siddhartha learned the skills he would need to be a king and a warrior, including archery, fencing and horse-riding. When

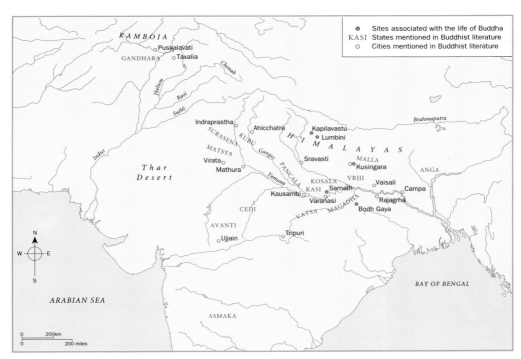

The main cities in northern India and Nepal at the time of Siddhartha's birth. Siddhartha grew up at his father's palace in Kapilavastu.

he was 16, according to the legend, he married Yashodhara, a princess from a neighbouring kingdom. Following the custom of the time, he won her hand in an archery contest.

The Four Sights

For many years, Siddhartha lived in great comfort. Under the king's careful supervision, he led a very sheltered life and never witnessed any kind of suffering. When he was 29 years old, however, he had an experience that changed his life. Disobeying his father's orders, he rode his chariot outside the walls of the palace. There he saw an old person, an ill person and a corpse. He had never seen such suffering before and was deeply shocked. Then he saw a wandering holy man. This man had given up his home and material possessions but still looked happy and contented.

This stone carving from Cambodia shows the birth of Siddhartha Gautama, who later became the Buddha, in the garden in Lumbini, Nepal.

Siddhartha decided to follow the holy man's example and dedicate his life to the search for a way to end suffering. That night he left home secretly, cut off his long hair and exchanged his fine clothes for rags. From that time on, he would live as a wandering holy man with no money, belongings or home.

SIDDHARTHA AND HINDUISM

When Siddhartha was born, the main religion in north-west India was Hinduism. Siddhartha may have been brought up as a Hindu, although no one is sure. Later, as the Buddha, he criticized the power of the upper-class Hindu priests and the formal nature of Hinduism, which seemed to exclude ordinary people. The Buddha taught that his path was open to everyone. It did not matter if people were rich or poor, what jobs they did, or which part of society they belonged to.

Searching for the truth

Siddhartha spent time with two religious teachers, learning how to meditate. He then spent six years living in the forest with a group of five holy men. They lived very hard lives, believing that this was the way to wisdom. Siddhartha underwent a series of terrible hardships (see panel opposite) but they did not help him on his quest.

Enlightenment Eventually, exhausted and weak, Siddhartha left his companions and made his way to the village of Bodh Gaya in north-east India. One evening, he sat down underneath a tall Bodhi tree to meditate, vowing not to move until he had discovered the truth. According to the legend, during the night Siddhartha was visited by Mara, the 'evil one', who tried to tempt him away from his quest. But nothing that Mara could say or do could disturb Siddhartha's resolve and, as the night drew on, he finally found the answers he had been looking for. He realized the truth about why people suffered and how

he could help them. He had become the Buddha, 'the Enlightened One'.

The first teaching After his enlightenment, the Buddha spent several days thinking over his experiences and continuing to meditate. He felt a deep sense of peace and joyfulness. It was during this time that he found his first followers – two passing merchants who brought him food. He decided to pass on what he had learnt to his original meditation teachers, but on discovering they were now dead, he went to find the five holy men who had been his companions in the forest. He found them in the deer park in Sarnath in northern India. He gave the holy men his first teaching, explaining the cause of suffering. This teaching is called the Four Noble Truths. The Buddha taught that everyone experiences suffering in life and that this suffering is caused by people not being content with what they have. There is, however, a way to end suffering, and this is by following the Noble Eightfold Path.

THE NOBLE EIGHTFOLD PATH

Buddha had learned that neither luxury nor hardship led to happiness. He taught a middle path, called the Noble Eightfold Path, between these two extremes. There are eight parts to the path:

1. Right understanding: seeing things in a detached way with a flexible, open mind, avoiding delusion or prejudice.
2. Right intention: ridding yourself of qualities you know to be wrong or immoral.
3. Right speech: abstaining from lying, from divisive or abusive speech, and from idle chatter.
4. Right action: not stealing, killing or performing any actions that might harm or upset other people.
5. Right livelihood: earning a living in a way that does not harm others.
6. Right effort: making an effort to be kind and compassionate and to avoid wrong or harmful actions.
7. Right mindfulness: being aware of your actions and thoughts.
8. Right concentration: training your mind to be calm and clear.

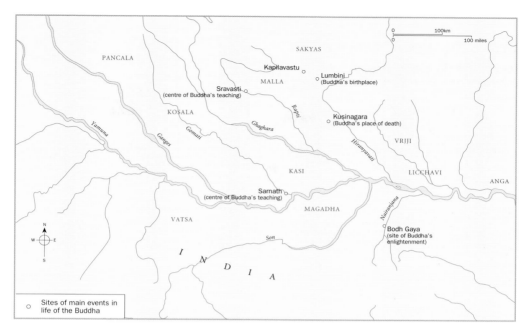

Above: *The sites of the key events in the Buddha's life. He was born in Lumbini, gained enlightenment in Bodh Gaya, gave his first teaching in Sarnath and died in Kushinagara.*

GREAT HARDSHIPS

I took food only once a day, or one in two or seven days. I lived on the roots and fruits of the forest, eating only those which fell of their own accord. I wore coarse clothes and rags from a rubbish heap. I became one who always stands and never sits. I made my bed on thorns. The dust and dirt of the years accumulated on my body. Because I ate so little, my limbs became like the knotted joints of withered creepers, my backbone stuck out like a row of beads and my ribs like the rafters of a tumble-down shed.

From the *Maha-Saccaka Suttas*

Left: *The Mahabodhi Temple in Bodh Gaya, India, where the Buddha gained enlightenment, is topped by a 50-metre high, pyramid-shaped spire. Inside the temple is a large, gilded image of the Buddha.*

Establishing the sangha

The Buddha spent the next 45 years travelling around north-east India, teaching people from all walks of life. Many of his followers dedicated their lives to Buddhism. They became monks and nuns and were known as the *sangha*. (For some Buddhists, the sangha also includes laypeople.) During this time, the Buddha helped many others gain enlightenment. These people became *arahats*, or 'worthy ones', and were sent out by the Buddha to teach. Among them was the Buddha's own father. The Buddha's only son, Rahula, was ordained as a monk.

Passing away

At the age of 80, the Buddha passed away. He had fallen ill with food poisoning and died in a grove of trees near the city of Kushinagara in northern India. Before he died, he told the monks not to be sad but reminded them of the teaching that everything changes and passes away. The Buddha did not name a successor but told the monks that his teachings should be their guide from now on. After the Buddha's death, the monks held a six-day ceremony in his honour and then cremated his body. His ashes were divided into eight and given to eight different rulers, who built dome-shaped monuments called *stupas* over the relics.

The First Buddhist Council

The Buddha's teachings were not written down during his lifetime. Instead, they were memorized by his followers and passed on by word of mouth. According to tradition, shortly after the Buddha's death, a council of 500 monks was called at the village of Rajagrha in north-eastern India to agree on the content of the teachings. Two collections of teachings were recited from memory by two of the most senior monks, Upali and Ananda. It is believed that these two collections represented the authentic

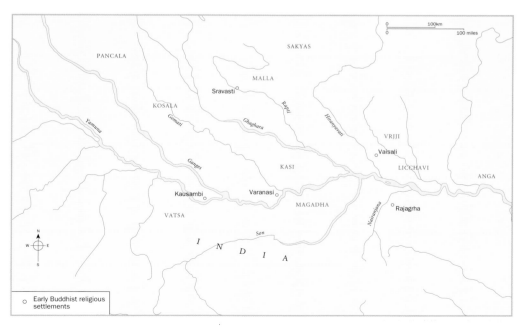

Early Buddhist religious settlements in northern India. These were important centres for Buddhist teaching, both by the Buddha himself and the sangha *of monks.*

teachings of the Buddha. However, the collections were not written down for several centuries.

The Second Buddhist Council

Around a hundred years after the first Buddhist Council, a Second Council was held in the city of Vesali in north-east India. Over the years, differences in practice and teaching had begun to emerge. This was not really surprising as the sangha was not a single group but was made up of many self-contained units with different schools of thought. The main dispute at the Second Council regarded the rules for how monks and nuns should live. Some groups of monks followed the rules less strictly than others; for example, they would accept money instead of gifts of food.

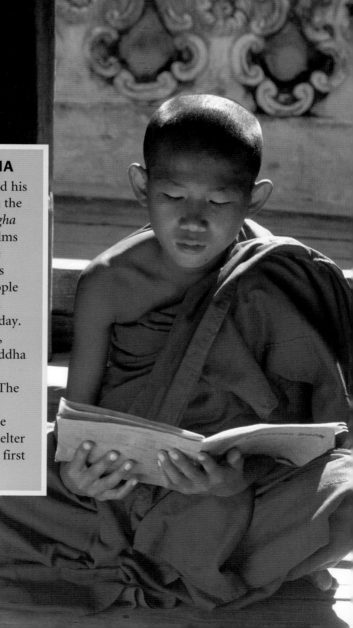

LIFE OF THE SANGHA

The daily life of the Buddha and his monks and nuns is recorded in the Buddhist sacred texts. The *sangha* possessed only a robe and an alms bowl. In the morning they rose early and began their daily alms rounds, during which local people gave them food and other gifts. They ate their one meal at midday. In the afternoons and evenings, they listened to talks by the Buddha or another senior monk, then meditated long into the night. The sangha moved constantly from place to place, except during the rainy season when they took shelter in buildings, which became the first monasteries.

Many Buddhists have followed in the Buddha's footsteps and became monks like him. This young monk is studying the sacred texts in a monastery in Myanmar (Burma).

A split develops At the second Buddhist Council, or perhaps some time later, this disagreement led the sangha to split into two groups, or schools: the Theravada, 'those who follow the way of the elders', and the Mahasanghika, 'the great assembly' and the forerunner of the Mahayana (see panel, right).

Buddhism spreads In the centuries after his death, the Buddha's followers continued to spread his teaching throughout India and beyond, and missionaries were sent into other Asian countries where they established thriving Buddhist communities. At the same time, many foreign monks came to study at the great Buddhist universities of India. During this period, Buddhism became the main religion in much of India, often with the support of Indian and foreign kings.

According to tradition, the Buddha was lying on his side when he passed away. This is called the parinirvana *(passing into nirvana).*

TWO GREAT SCHOOLS

Theravada Buddhists claim that the pure teachings of the Buddha, unchanged for centuries, are recorded in a scripture called the Tipitaka. They believe that the Buddha was a human being, although a very special one. Mahayana Buddhists follow the teachings of the Buddha but also of other enlightened Buddhist teachers, and they have many additional sacred texts. They also worship mythical, god-like figures known as *bodhisattvas* who, out of compassion, choose to help other people to overcome suffering. Theravada Buddhism spread south to Sri Lanka, Myanmar, Laos, Thailand and Cambodia. Mahayana Buddhism spread north to Tibet, China, Korea, Japan and Vietnam.

This standing Buddha from Gandhara shows the mixture of Indian and Greek styles.

The first-ever images of the Buddha were produced by Gandharan craftsmen from around the first century CE. Before this, the Buddha had not been depicted in person but through symbols such as an empty throne, a stupa, a Bodhi tree, a footprint or an animal. The style of these early images was strongly influenced by Greek art. Gandharan craftspeople blended Indian and Greek styles to produce graceful

Gandhara In 326 BCE, the Macedonian general Alexander the Great conquered the north-western part of India. A Hellenistic kingdom called Gandhara was established in the area. Buddhist missionaries were soon at work in the region, eventually gaining the support of local rulers such as King Milinda (see panel). Gandhara reached its height from the first to the fifth centuries CE under the Buddhist Kushan kings (see page 151). It was also the location of the first great Buddhist university, in the town of Taxila, which attracted Buddhist scholars from far and wide and became an important base for Buddhist missionaries travelling into Central Asia. Gandhara survived until the 11th century, when it was conquered by Muslim invaders.

MILINDA'S QUESTIONS

Many of the Greek rulers were influenced by Buddhism, including King Milinda (ruled 155–130 BCE). Milinda (the Indian version of the Greek name Menandros) is said to have had a famous debate about Buddhism with the great teacher and monk Nagasena. The king asked Nagasena a series of questions about the Buddha's teaching. Afterwards, it is said, he was so impressed that he converted to Buddhism. The debate is recorded in an important Buddhist text called 'The Questions of King Milinda'.

statues draped in long, flowing robes. Traders passing through Gandhara took this art with them on their travels into Central Asia and China.

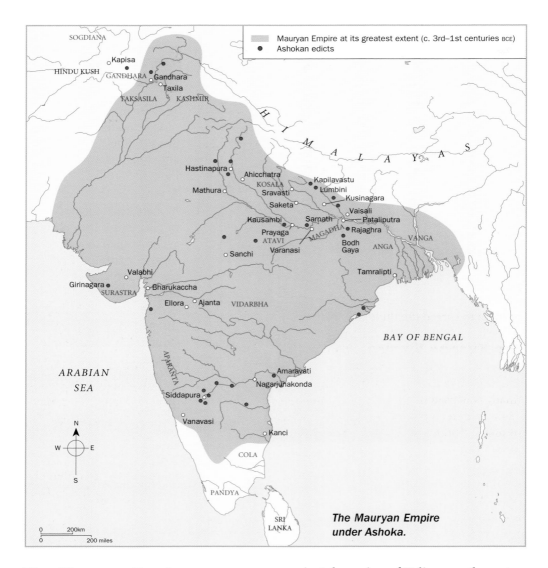

The Mauryan Empire
under Ashoka.

The Mauryan Empire

In around 321 BCE, a leader called Chandragupta Maurya conquered the area of northern India where the Buddha had taught and founded the great Mauryan Empire. Chandragupta established his capital at Pataliputra (the modern-day city of Patna). The empire reached its greatest extent under his grandson Ashoka (ruled 265–232 BCE). Soon, most of India, apart from the extreme south, had come under Mauryan rule. In around 260 BCE, Ashoka launched a particularly ruthless campaign against the region of Kalinga on the east coast. It was one of the few places in India to resist the Mauryans. According to some accounts, 100,000 people were killed in the battle and thousands more were injured or taken prisoner. Afterwards, Ashoka was filled with remorse. To make amends, he converted to Buddhism.

Ashoka and Buddhism

Ashoka became the greatest patron and supporter of Buddhism in ancient India. During his rule, all the existing Buddhist centres were expanded greatly, and new monasteries and stupas were built. More importantly, Ashoka vowed to establish a society based not on war and violence but on the Buddhist principles of compassion and peace. He himself tried to set an example. He travelled widely through the empire listening to people's opinions about what would make their lives easier. In response, he built much-needed wells and reservoirs, set up free hospitals for the poor, planted trees and provided welfare services for prisoners. He gave up hunting, his favourite sport, and instead went on pilgrimages to holy places linked with the Buddha's life. He also sent missionaries out of India to spread the Buddha's teaching.

The Kushan Empire
After Ashoka's death in 231 BCE, the Mauryan Empire began to break up and finally collapsed in 184 BCE. After a period of unrest, India was invaded by the Scythian people from Central Asia, who founded the Kushan Empire. Their king, Kanishka (ruled c. 78–102 CE), was a keen supporter of Buddhism, and in about 100 CE, he called Buddhists together for a Fourth Council in Kashmir. (The Third Council, ordered by Ashoka, had taken place in around 250 BCE in Pataliputra.) Since the collapse of the Mauryan Empire, Buddhism had split into 18 different schools. The aim of the Fourth Council was to try to bring these different schools together and to approve a new set of scriptures, written in Sanskrit, the ancient religious language of India. These scriptures became associated with the Mahayana school.

ASHOKA'S EDICTS

Throughout his empire, Ashoka had a series of edicts carved onto rock faces and sandstone pillars. These were written in the ancient Indian language of Magadhi and were deciphered for the first time in 1837 by British scholar James Prinsep. They were placed at the borders of the empire and in places connected with the Buddha. Some edicts told of Ashoka's conversion to Buddhism. Others explained the Buddha's teachings and told people to behave accordingly, by living responsible and moral lives, helping others, being generous and truthful, and not killing or harming living beings. Special officers were appointed to travel through the empire explaining the Buddha's teachings.

The Lion Capital of Ashoka, once on a pillar, now in the museum at Sarnath.

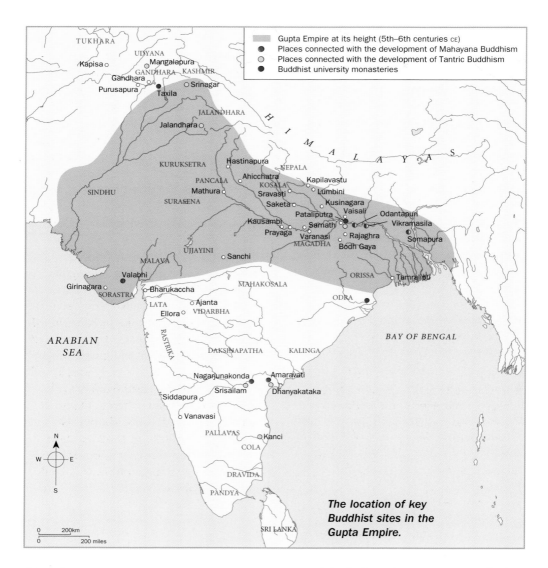

The location of key Buddhist sites in the Gupta Empire.

Map legend:
- Gupta Empire at its height (5th–6th centuries CE)
- Places connected with the development of Mahayana Buddhism
- Places connected with the development of Tantric Buddhism
- Buddhist university monasteries

The Gupta Empire With the decline of the Kushan Empire, Chandra Gupta I (320–c. 330 CE) established the Gupta Empire across northern India. Under the Guptas, a golden age of Indian culture and history began. Literature, art and religion flourished, and even though the Guptas largely followed the Hindu religion, Buddhism was given royal support. Great Buddhist universities were established at Nalanda (see panel) and in other locations. New Buddhist texts were written, and many fine works of art were created, including the paintings inside the Buddhist cave temples at Ajanta in western India, which can still be seen today. The Gupta Empire lasted until the sixth century CE when it was attacked by the Huns, a people from Central Asia.

Buddhism declines The Huns destroyed many Buddhist centres in north-west India, including Taxila. Over the next few centuries, Buddhism survived but no longer enjoyed royal support. But it was the series of devastating raids by Muslims from Afghanistan from the 11th century onwards that finally ended 1,700 years of Buddhism in India. The non-violent nature of Buddhism made it an easy target for the Muslim armies. Monasteries were destroyed, and, in 1199, Nalanda was burnt to the ground and its monks slaughtered. Since then, in India Buddhism has never really recovered, and Hinduism remains the country's principal religion. India still attracts Buddhist pilgrims from all over the world to visit its sacred sites, but as recently as 1991, only one per cent of Indians considered themselves Buddhist.

NALANDA UNIVERSITY

The greatest university in the Buddhist world was at Nalanda (in modern Bihar). It may have already been in existence in the Buddha's lifetime. In its heyday in the fifth century CE, it attracted over 10,000 students and 1,500 teachers from all over India and Asia. Subjects included the study of the Buddhist scriptures, Hinduism, philosophy, astronomy, mathematics and medicine. Among Nalanda's most famous teachers was the monk Nagarjuna (c. second century CE), who founded the influential Madhyamaka (Middle Path) school of Mahayana Buddhism. His main teaching was on the Buddhist concept of *sunyata* (emptiness), the idea that nothing exists on its own, and that everything is dependent on other things and causes.

Sri Lanka Although Buddhism declined in its heartland of India, it flourished elsewhere, thanks mainly to the endeavours of Ashoka many centuries earlier. Ashoka sent out missionary monks to spread the Buddha's teachings. The first country they came to, in about 250 BCE, was the island of Sri Lanka.

The missionaries were supposedly led by Ashoka's own son, Mahinda, who had become a Buddhist monk. He converted King Tissa to Buddhism, and it quickly took root on the island, becoming the major religion. Later, Ashoka's daughter, the nun Sanghamitta, visited Sri Lanka, taking with her a cutting from the original Bodhi tree under which the Buddha gained enlightenment. It was planted in the capital Anuradhapura, where it still grows today.

During the second century BCE, Tamil invaders from India ruled parts of Sri Lanka and Buddhism suffered. Many monks fled or died. It was about this time that the Tipitaka was written down to prevent it from being lost, since there were no longer enough monks who could remember it all.

The ruins of the great Buddhist university of Nalanda in Bihar, India.

Between the first and seventh centuries CE, Buddhism thrived in Sri Lanka. From the seventh to 12th centuries, however, South Indian kings invaded the island and Buddhism declined. In 1070, King Vijayabahu (ruled 1055–1110) recaptured the island and set about restoring Buddhism, but it was in such a poor state that he had to bring in an order of monks from Myanmar to form a new sangha. In the 12th century, King Parakramabahu (ruled 1153–1186) built many magnificent Buddhist monasteries and stupas in the new capital of Polonnaruwa.

With the arrival of Europeans on the island in the 16th and 17th centuries, Buddhism suffered again as they tried to

RIVAL MONASTERIES

King Tissa built the Mahavihara (Great Monastery) for Mahinda and his monks at Anuradhapura. The Mahavihara became the headquarters of Theravada Buddhism. But in the first century BCE, the monks' position was threatened when another great monastery, the Abhayagiri, was built. The Abhayagiri became associated with Mahayana Buddhism, and a fierce rivalry began between the two monasteries. Mahayana Buddhism did not achieve a lasting hold in Sri Lanka, however, and by the 12th century the Abhayagiri had declined. Sri Lanka remains a Theravada country.

convert the islanders to Christianity. There was another revival in the 18th century when several new orders of monks were formed.

From 1796 to 1948, Sri Lanka was part of the British Empire, attracting followers who helped to spread Buddhism to the West.

Today, after 2,300 years, Sri Lanka remains a proudly Buddhist country and the homeland of the Theravada tradition. Some 80 per cent of the islanders are Sinhalese, most of whom are Buddhists. With

A Buddhist shrine at Mihintale, Sri Lanka, where Mahinda met the king of the island.

An image of the seated Buddha next to a stupa on the upper terrace at Borobodur. The monument has over 400 Buddha images.

some 15,000 monks on the island, the sangha remains at the centre of Buddhist life, and the monks are held in great respect by the community.

Indonesia According to tradition, the first Buddhists to reach South-East Asia were missionaries sent by Ashoka in the third century BCE. They travelled sea trade routes to the 'Land of Gold' – probably the west coast of Indonesia. Buddhism really began to make an impact in Indonesia in the first century CE, by which time many Indians had settled there.

Between about 600 and 800 CE, Sumatra was ruled by the mainly Buddhist city-state of Srivijaya where Theravada communities were already present, although Mahayana communities arrived soon after. The great Indian Buddhist teacher, Atisha, studied in Srivijaya in the 12th century, and students travelled from Indonesia to study at Nalanda University. Indonesia was also a regular stopping point for Chinese Buddhist monks on their way to India. In Java, both Buddhism and Hinduism attracted followers, with Buddhism becoming the dominant religion. In the eighth century, the Shailendra kings came to power and were strong patrons of Mahayana Buddhism. Their capital at Palembang became a great centre of Buddhist learning. In around 800 CE, the Shailendras sponsored the building of Borobodur (see panel, above).

From the 13th century, Islam became the major religion of Indonesia, although a mixture of Buddhism and Hinduism still survives in Bali and in parts of Java. In the 20th century, Buddhism enjoyed a revival, and there are now around three million Buddhists in Indonesia.

Myanmar Buddhism did not become well established in Burma, present-day Myanmar, until the Mon period, from the fifth to the 10th centuries CE. The Mon people of southern Myanmar followed the Theravada tradition, as did the Pyu people of central Myanmar. Mahayana Buddhism may have arrived earlier than Theravada, but it did not take hold.

In the 11th century, King Anuruddha (ruled 1044–1077) overthrew the Mon and unified the country. During his rule, Theravada Buddhism became firmly established. Anuruddha built his capital at Pagan, which is still famous for its amazing Buddhist ruins. Myanmar was

MYANMAR TODAY

Buddhism remains the national religion of Myanmar, practised by about 85 per cent of the population. Despite the country's harsh military government, Buddhism continues to thrive, with thousands of monks and nuns, and some 6,000 monasteries.

later invaded by the Thais, who adopted Theravada Buddhism. In 1886, the country became part of the British Empire. For many people in Myanmar, Buddhism became a powerful symbol of national identity during the periods when they were ruled by foreign powers.

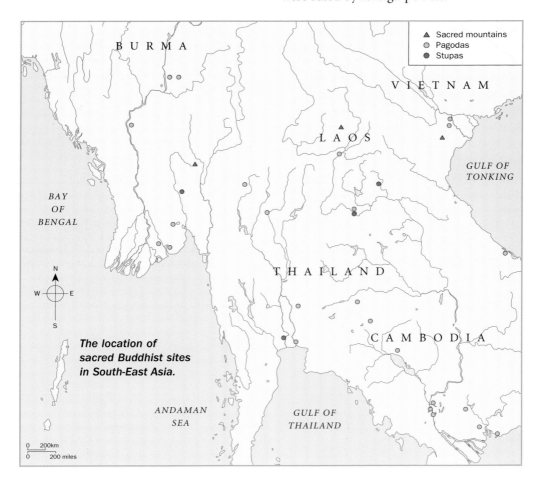

The location of sacred Buddhist sites in South-East Asia.

Vietnam, Cambodia and Laos

Theravada missionaries may have reached Vietnam by sea as early as the second century CE, but the story of Buddhism in Vietnam really begins in 580 CE. An Indian monk, Vinitaruci, who had studied in China, arrived in Vietnam bringing Mahayana Buddhism with him. Mahayana quickly took hold in Vietnam and when the country was unified in 939 CE, it became the national religion. Two schools of Chinese Mahayana Buddhism – Chan (Zen) and Pure Land – became particularly popular. Buddhism was well supported by the Vietnamese kings, who regularly appointed monks to key positions at court. Over the following centuries, Buddhism became closely linked with Vietnamese nationalism. From 1883 to 1954, Vietnam came under French rule, and two Buddhist movements played a part in the struggle for independence: the Central Vietnamese Buddhist Association and the General Association of Buddhism in Vietnam.

In the ninth century CE, Cambodia had strong links with both India and China, but its Khmer rulers preferred Hinduism to Buddhism. This changed, however, with the reign of King Jayavarman VII (ruled 1181–c. 1215). He converted to Mahayana Buddhism, and the country became Buddhist. From the early 13th century, Cambodia suffered a series of invasions by the Thais. Thereafter, possibly under the influence of the invaders, the kings of Cambodia became Theravada Buddhists. During this time, the neighbouring country of Laos fell under the control of the Khmer, the Thais and Myanmar. When Laos regained its independence in 1350, Theravada Buddhism was introduced, and the king invited monks from Cambodia and Sri Lanka to his court to act as his advisors.

Thailand

The Thai kingdom of Sukhothai, which lasted from the early 1100s to 1350 CE, adopted Theravada Buddhism from Myanmar. But it was not until the kingdom of Ayutthaya was founded in 1350 that Buddhism became the state religion, with the king as head of the sangha. Later kings continued to protect, support and reform Buddhism. King Rama IV (ruled 1851–1868) spent 25 years as a monk before ascending the throne. He revised the sacred texts and founded a new order of monks. King Rama V (ruled 1868–1910) continued these policies and passed three 'Sangha Acts', setting out the duties of monks, particularly in the areas of healthcare and education.

A young monk in Thailand collects alms from a Thai Buddhist outside a monastery. Buddhism remains very strong in Thailand.

The close ties between the Thai king and the sangha continue today. The king no longer has so much power but is still the honorary head of the sangha. Meanwhile, the government supervises the organization of the sangha. Buddhism remains very strong in Thailand, even as the country becomes more Westernized. Some 94 per cent of the population are Buddhists. Many Thai men spend time in the sangha as part of their education. This has helped to strengthen the relationship between lay Buddhists and the sangha.

China Buddhism reached China around the first century CE, probably spread by merchants travelling from India via Central Asia along the great trade route known as the Silk Road. It was not readily accepted at first. The Chinese already had their own established religious traditions – principally Confucianism and Taoism. However, some Buddhist texts were translated into Chinese, and Chinese

Stone sculptures from the Longmen Caves, one of the most important Buddhist sites in China.

people began to join the sangha. Taoism remained popular with the aristocracy, but Buddhism appealed to ordinary people. By the fourth century CE, there were 24,000 Buddhist monks and almost 2,000 monasteries in China.

The sixth to the ninth centuries CE were a golden age for Chinese Buddhism. During this period, many different

PILGRIM MONKS

To collect Buddhist texts for translation into Chinese, several Chinese monks made long, gruelling journeys to India. Fa-hsien (338–422 CE) set off in 399. He finally reached India after crossing the Takla Makan Desert and the Pamir Mountains, which were said to shelter dragons that spat out poison. More than 200 years later, another monk, Hsuan-tsang (602–664 CE) followed in Fa Hsien's footsteps. Hsuan Tsang visited many Buddhist sites in India, including Nalanda University, and brought back so many texts that he needed 20 horses to carry them all.

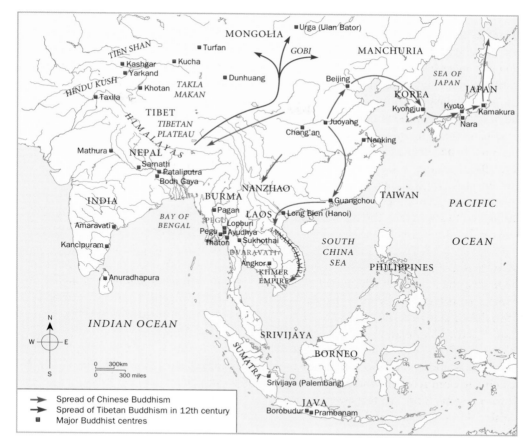

The spread of Chinese Buddhism
Spread of Tibetan Buddhism in 12th century
Major Buddhist centres

schools of Chinese Mahayana Buddhism developed. In the ninth century, a backlash began against the power and wealth of the Buddhist monasteries. Buddhism survived but was greatly weakened. In the 12th century, it lost ground to Confucianism, which became the official state religion.

Two of the most popular schools of Chinese Buddhism were Ching t'u (Pure Land) and Chan (Zen in Japanese). Pure Land is based on the worship of the Buddha Amitabha, who is believed to live in a heavenly place called the Pure Land. If people have faith in Amitabha and chant his name, they will be reborn in the Pure Land. From there they will be able to progress easily towards enlightenment. Tradition says that Chan was brought to

The spread of Buddhism to China, Japan and Korea.

China by the Indian monk Bodhidharma in the early sixth century CE. It uses meditation as a means of experiencing reality and seeing the world as it really is.

In 1949, China came under Communist rule. The Communists suppressed Buddhism and other religions harshly. This persecution was particularly brutal during the Cultural Revolution (1966–1969) when Buddhism was practically wiped out. In the 1980s, some Buddhist temples were rebuilt and Buddhist organizations revived. This revival was halted in the late 1980s, however, when the Communist government cracked down on Buddhism again.

Korea Buddhism was introduced to Korea in the fourth century CE by Chinese monks. They brought with them Buddhist texts and images and built several monasteries. Under the Silla Dynasty (618–935 CE), Buddhism received royal support, helping it to flourish. Silla monks travelled to China and India to bring back the latest teachings. Buddhism continued to thrive under the Koryo dynasty (918–1392). The first ruler, King T'aejo, was a devout Buddhist who built ten great monasteries in

CHINUL AND CHOGYE

One of the most important Korean Buddhists was the monk Chinul (1158–1210). He became a Son (Chan) monk when he was seven years old. Chinul passed all his monastic examinations, but instead of rising to a high position in the sangha, he decided to form his own Buddhist school. It was called the Chogye school and attracted many followers, including the king. When Chinul opened his Suson Monastery in 1205, the king declared 120 days of national celebrations. Chogye remains the main Korean school, and the Suson Monastery continues to be a major centre of Korean Buddhism.

Colourful lanterns hanging outside the Pulguk-sa Buddhist Temple in Kyongu, Korea.

1910 to 1945, Korea came under Japanese control. Monasteries were divided up and there were conflicts between different groups of monks. The monk Han Yongun (1879–1944)

his capital. Senior monks were appointed as royal advisors and it was usual for members of the royal family to become monks. A new edition of the Korean scriptures, amounting to over 5,000 volumes, was collected and printed, and the monasteries became very rich and powerful.

Their powers were greatly reduced during the Choson dynasty (1392–1910) when stricter rules were drawn up for the monks. Even so, Buddhism continued to enjoy royal support for many years. From

campaigned hard to protect Korean Buddhism. After World War II, the country was divided into North Korea and South Korea. The Communist government in the north stamped down on religion, and Buddhism was almost wiped out, but in the south, Buddhism remains strong.

Japan Mahayana Buddhism reached Japan from Korea in the sixth century CE. A Korean king sent a mission to the Japanese emperor, which included

Buddhist monks carrying texts and images of the Buddha. Under Prince Shotoku (ruled 574–622), Buddhism flourished in Japan, existing alongside Shinto, the ancient Japanese religion. Shotoku built Buddhist temples and monasteries and made Buddhism the state religion. In the eighth century, two forms of Chinese Buddhism – Tendai and Shingon – became popular. Both had mountain-top monasteries as their Japanese headquarters. In the 12th and 13th centuries, new schools developed, including Zen. Zen monasteries played an important role in protecting the teachings of Buddhism during the unsettled 14th and 15th centuries when many wars were fought between rival warlords. The 16th and 17th centuries saw the arrival of Christian missionaries in Japan. To preserve Buddhism, the emperor ordered all Japanese people, religious or not, to register with a Buddhist monastery.

One of the greatest teachers of Japanese Buddhism was the monk Nichiren (1222–1282). He trained at the great Tendai monastery on Mount Hiei outside Kyoto, but left to form his own school of Buddhism. He simplified the Tendai teachings to focus on the *Lotus Sutra*, one of the key Mahayana texts, and taught his followers that by simply chanting the name of the Lotus Sutra, they could purify their minds. Nichiren was frequently persecuted because of his outspoken attacks on other Buddhist groups. He escaped execution but was banished to a remote island. Despite this, Nichiren's influence remains strong to this day, and several modern Japanese Buddhist groups follow his teachings.

The great Buddha statue at Kamakura in Japan dates from the 13th century.

In the 19th century, Shinto became the state religion of Japan, and remained so until 1945. But Buddhism continued to thrive. Today, about 75 per cent of Japanese people regard themselves as Buddhists. Many actually follow a mixture of Buddhism and Shinto, and in many places Buddhist temples and Shinto shrines stand side by side. In addition, many new religious groups have sprung up. These are based on ancient Buddhist teachings but in a different form. They include Soka-gakkai, which is a form of Nichiren Buddhism.

A Tibetan Buddhist monk reads the sacred texts.

Early Tibetan Buddhism

The story of Buddhism in Tibet begins with King Songsten Gampo (ruled c. 609–650 CE), the founder of the Tibetan Empire. Two of his wives, a Nepalese princess and a Chinese princess, were devout Buddhists. It is unclear whether the king himself converted to Buddhism, but he built two magnificent Buddhist temples, the Jokhang and the Rampoche, for his wives. These housed two statues of the Buddha that they had brought with them as dowries.

King Khrisong Detsen (ruled 755–797), later made Buddhism the state religion, but not without opposition – a long struggle began between Buddhism and Bon, the established religion of Tibet at the time. King Ralpachan (ruled 817–836) went even further and became a Buddhist monk. He was assassinated by his brother, Langdarma, a strong supporter of Bon.

Langdarma persecuted the Buddhists, destroying monasteries and killing monks. In 842, however, he himself was killed by a Buddhist monk. In the 10th and 11th centuries, many monks fled to Tibet from India to escape Muslim attacks. As a result, Tibetan Buddhism revived and flourished.

Translating texts

King Songsten Gampo sent a translator to India to create an alphabet for the Tibetan language, which had not yet been written down. This enabled Buddhist sacred texts from India to be translated from Sanskrit into Tibetan. Over several centuries, Tibetan translators created a huge collection of holy books. Tibetan texts are placed into two main groups – the *Kanjur* and the *Tenjur*. The *Kanjur* has 108 volumes and contains the words of the Buddha. The *Tenjur* has 360 volumes and contains commentaries on the *Kanjur* texts. This work also helped

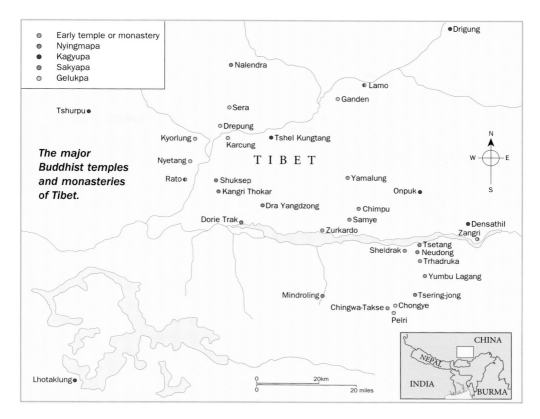

The major Buddhist temples and monasteries of Tibet.

TIBET

Drigung
Nalendra
Lamo
Ganden
Tshurpu
Sera
Drepung
Kyorlung
Karcung
Tshel Kungtang
Nyetang
Rato
Shuksep
Yamalung
Kangri Thokar
Onpuk
Dra Yangdzong
Chimpu
Dorie Trak
Samye
Zurkardo
Densathil
Zangri
Sheldrak
Tsetang
Neudong
Trhadruka
Yumbu Lagang
Mindroling
Tsering-jong
Chingwa-Takse
Chongye
Pelri
Lhotaklung

CHINA
NEPAL
INDIA
BURMA

to preserve the original Indian texts, as Buddhism declined in India.

Tantric Buddhism A unique form of Buddhism is practised in Tibet, known as tantric Buddhism. Tantric Buddhism is a type of Mahayana Buddhism that uses magic spells and rituals to help people gain enlightenment. It gets its name from a collection of mysterious sacred texts called the *Tantras* and was introduced into Tibet by Padmasambhava. Tantric Buddhism is sometimes called Vajrayana, which means 'thunderbolt' in Sanskrit, because it is seen as a particularly swift path to enlightenment.

PADMASAMBHAVA, 'LOTUS BORN'

In the late eighth century, the famous Indian teacher, Padmasambhava, arrived in Tibet. He helped establish Buddhism among the ordinary Tibetan people. Padmasambhava's name means 'lotus born', and legend says that he was born from a lotus flower. He was considered a saint with amazing magical powers. According to tradition, King Khrisong Detsen organized a magic contest between Padmasambhava and the most powerful Bon priests and their demon allies. Padmasambhava is said to have used spectacular feats of magic to overcome them and convert them to Buddhism. During Padmasambhava's time, the first Buddhist monastery was built at Samye, and the first Tibetans became monks.

Different schools

From the ninth century, several different schools of Tibetan Buddhism developed. The oldest is the Nyingmapa tradition, which traces its teachings back to Padmasambhava. He is thought to have buried a collection of sacred texts in the mountains in preparation for the time when people would be ready for their teachings. The Kadampa tradition was founded by another Indian monk, Atisha (982–1054). It stressed discipline and morality and had strict rules for its monks. The followers of another school, the Sakyapas, were named after the grey colour of the earth around their monastery. They became very powerful in the 12th and 13th centuries.

By the 13th century, Buddhism was flourishing in Tibet. Several of the Buddhist schools became involved in politics. In 1240, the Mongols from the north-west threatened to invade Tibet. In an effort to protect the country, the head of the Sakyapas, Sakya Pandita (1182–1251), travelled to the Mongol court. He offered to become spiritual advisor to the Mongol leader in return for Tibet being left in peace. The plan worked and the Sakyapas became the effective rulers of Tibet.

By the early 15th century, however,

power had passed to another school, the Gelukpas, founded in 1409 by the Tibetan teacher Tsong-Kha-pa (1357–1419). He built the great monasteries of Ganden, Drepung and Sera for his followers. In their heyday, these monasteries were like small cities, housing tens of thousands of monks. In the 16th century, the leader of the Gelukpas was given the title Dalai Lama by the Mongols. The title means 'ocean of wisdom', meaning someone whose wisdom is as deep as the ocean.

An image of the bodhisattva, *Avalokitesvara. Tibetans believe that the Dalai Lama is Avalokitesvara in human form.*

MARPA AND MILAREPA

The Tibetan Kagyupa school was founded by a great Buddhist teacher called Marpa (1012–1096). His disciple, Milarepa (1040–1123), became one of Tibet's most revered saints. Legend says he turned to Buddhism to make amends for using magic to punish his uncle. After his training with Marpa, Milarepa spent most of his life living in a lonely mountain cave. He dressed in rags and ate boiled nettles. Despite his harsh existence, Milarepa is famous for his collection of songs and poems, which tell of the joy of enlightenment. Known as *The Hundred Thousand Songs of Milarepa*, it remains one of the most popular sacred texts of Tibetan Buddhism.

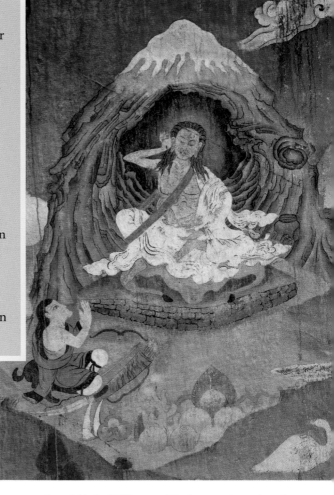

A painting of Milarepa, Tibetan saint, poet and yogi, in Tukang, Helambu, Nepal.

The Dalai Lamas

The title of Dalai Lama was first given to Sonam Gyatso (1543–1588), but he 'backdated' the honour to two previous Gelukpa leaders. Consequently, Gedun Truppa (1391–1475) is considered the first Dalai Lama. Tibetans believe that the Dalai Lama is the incarnation of the *bodhisattva*, Avalokitesvara, who deliberately chose to be reborn in human form in order to help other suffering beings. When a Dalai Lama dies, a search is made for a baby who is his next incarnation. He is known by various signs; for example, he may be able to recognize old friends from his previous incarnation, or to pick out belongings such as prayer beads. The baby is taken from his family and spends many years in Lhasa, the Tibetan capital, being educated.

By the 17th century, the Dalai Lama had become both the religious and the political leader of Tibet. The fifth Dalai Lama (1617–1682) built the famous Potala Palace in Lhasa. Over the following centuries, the Dalai Lamas were caught up in political intrigue, particularly over Chinese claims to Tibet, and were forced to give up some political power to the Chinese. This remained the situation until the 13th Dalai Lama (1875–1933) assumed full power and ruled Tibet until his death.

Chinese invasion In 1951, Chinese Communist forces invaded Tibet. At first, efforts were made to combine Communism with Buddhist religious freedom. But Communists objected to many Buddhist practices, and many Tibetans objected to Chinese rule. Thousands of monks were imprisoned or killed, and the teachings of Buddhism were outlawed. In 1959, after an unsuccessful Tibetan uprising, the 14th Dalai Lama was forced to flee from Lhasa in disguise. He settled in India where he was joined by some 100,000 fellow Tibetans. Those left behind suffered terribly. Worse was to follow during the Chinese Cultural Revolution of the 1960s. Buddhist temples and works of art were systematically destroyed, and the great monasteries were reduced to ghost towns. In the space of 20 years, a centuries-old way of life had been devastated.

Today, the Dalai Lama and his many Buddhist monks are based in Dharamsala, India, where they have established a thriving Tibetan community and government in exile. The town has several Buddhist monasteries and temples, a school of Tibetan studies and studios where traditional works of Tibetan Buddhist art are produced. Since 1980, the Chinese rulers have granted some limited religious freedom in Tibet, but the Dalai Lama has not been allowed to return, and Buddhism in Tibet faces a very uncertain future.

Engaged Buddhism Many Buddhists today, in Asia and beyond, are becoming involved in 'engaged Buddhism'. This means becoming involved, or engaged, in many aspects of social work, peace campaigning, politics and human rights. For example, Buddhists have set up hospitals and AIDS charities, visited prisons and led protests against the international arms trade. One famous

THE 14TH DALAI LAMA

The present Dalai Lama, Tenzin Gyatso (born 1935), is the 14th. He was taken to Lhasa at the age of five and made head of state at the age of 16. From his home in India, the Dalai Lama travels all over the world, campaigning for the rights of the Tibetan people. His warmth, wisdom and compassion have made him a much-loved and respected statesman. In 1989, he was awarded the Nobel Peace Prize for his work.

Tenzin Gyatso, the 14th Dalai Lama, at his home in Dharamsala, India.

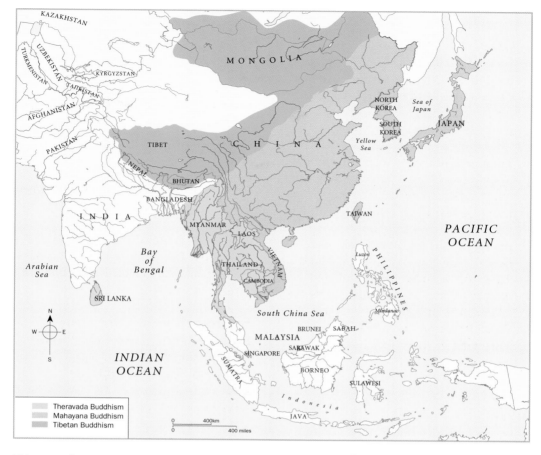

This map shows where different forms of Buddhism are practised in Asia today.

example of engaged Buddhism is the Wat Tham Krabok monastery in Thailand. Since 1957, the monks and nuns at this monastery have run a very strict but successful detoxification programme for drug addicts. The programme is based on Buddhist principles.

Buddhism in South-East Asia

Vietnam has been under Communist rule since the 1950s. But Buddhism has continued there alongside Communism, although the sangha is regulated by the government. In Cambodia, however, Buddhism was practically wiped out. From 1975 to 1979, a Communist movement called the Khmer Rouge held power. Under its leader, Pol Pot, many monasteries were destroyed and thousands of monks were tortured and killed. In 1979, a delegation of monks had to be sent from Vietnam to revive Cambodia's sangha. Today, Buddhism is officially the state religion of Cambodia, but its recovery is slow and its future still hangs in the balance.

In Thailand and Sri Lanka, Buddhism remains the major religion and continues to exercise a strong influence on society. The sangha plays a vital role, as it has for centuries. Monks are involved in education, health and social work, and conservation. They act as spiritual advisors to local communities, helping people to live according to Buddhist principles.

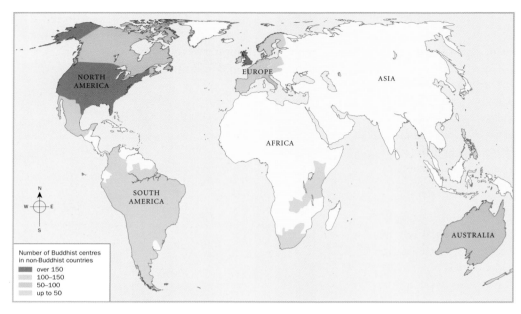

Buddhist centres in non-traditional Buddhist countries outside Asia.

Buddhism in India

Although Hinduism and Islam are today the major religions of India, Buddhism has shown some signs of revival. This is largely thanks to the work of Dr B. R. Ambedkar (1891–1956), an Indian lawyer and politician. He was born into a Dalit family, the lowest rank of Indian Hindu society. Hostility against his campaigns for equal rights for Dalits led Ambedkar to convert to Buddhism. Millions of other Dalits followed his example.

Buddhism in the West

Until about 100 years ago, very few people in the West had heard of Buddhism. But over the last century, Buddhism has grown rapidly and attracted thousands of followers. It has now become firmly established in Britain, the USA, Australia and in most European countries, and is becoming more popular in South America and Africa.

The British first made contact with Buddhism in the late 18th and early 19th century when the British Empire expanded to include Buddhist countries such as Burma (Myanmar) and Sri Lanka. Some of the first Westerners to study Buddhism were British civil servants working in these countries. Other Buddhist countries, such as Vietnam and Cambodia, came under French rule and French scholars also began to study Buddhism.

In 1879, Edward Arnold, a British teacher in India, published a poem called 'The Light of Asia', based on the Buddha's life, which helped to spread an awareness of the Buddha. In 1881, British scholar T. W. Rhys Davids (1843–1922) founded the Pali Text Society. The society collected Theravada Buddhist texts and translated them, making Buddhism accessible to many more people in the West.

At the start of the 20th century, the first Westerners became Buddhist monks. Among them was Briton Alan Bennett (1873–1923). He was ordained in Burma and took the Buddhist name Ananda

Maitreya. Bennett helped found the first Buddhist society in Britain in 1908. In 1926, a Sri Lankan, Anagarika Dharmapala (1874–1933) founded a Buddhist centre in London, the first outside Asia. Buddhist societies were also formed in Germany (1903 and 1924) and France (1929). The Buddhist Society of America was established in 1930 in New York City.

Since then, interest in Buddhism has grown steadily, and new centres and societies open every year. There are currently over 100 centres in Britain and many more in the USA. Some are mainly for people who have emigrated from Asia; others cater for Westerners who want to learn meditation or follow a Buddhist way of life. There are also many Buddhist monasteries in the West, run by Western monks and nuns.

THE THEOSOPHICAL SOCIETY

An organization called the Theosophical Society helped introduce Buddhist ideas to the West. Founded in 1875 in New York by two Americans, Colonel Henry Steel Olcott (1832–1907) and Helena Blavatsky (1831–1891), it drew its ideas from many different ancient traditions, including Hinduism and Buddhism. Olcott and Blavatsky may have been the first Westerners to formally become Buddhists. On a visit to Sri Lanka in 1880, they visited a temple and pledged themselves to Buddhism in the presence of a Buddhist monk.

Madame Helena Petrovna Blavatsky (1831–1891).

Buddhist traditions in the West

Before the 1950s, almost the only type of Buddhism known in the West was Theravada. A Sri Lankan *vihara* (Buddhist temple) was set up in London in 1954, followed by a Thai vihara in 1966. In the mid-1950s, Japanese Zen Buddhism also became popular in Britain and the USA. In the 1960s and 1970s, Tibetan refugees set up centres in the USA, Britain, Europe and Australia. A Tibetan monk called Chogyam Trungpa established the Samye Ling Monastery in Scotland, and a Tibetan Buddhist centre in the USA. It is estimated that, today, about half of Western Buddhists follow a form of Tibetan Buddhism. Other smaller groups have become well established, such as Japanese Pure Land and Shingon. Modern Buddhist movements have also emerged, including Soka-gakkai, a branch of Nichiren Buddhism. Its teachings are based on daily chanting as a means not only to spiritual but also to material rewards. Many Buddhists have criticized its approach.

The New Kadampa movement

One of the fastest-growing Buddhist groups in the West is the New Kadampa tradition. Founded by the Tibetan monk Geshe Kelsang Gyatso Rinpoche, it has over 900 meditation centres in 40 countries. New Kadampa is based on Kadampa Buddhism, which dates back to 11th-century Tibet. It emphasizes moral discipline, study and meditation as ways to peace and happiness. Followers of New Kadampa also worship a spirit called Dorje Shugden. In 1998, the first New Kadampa temple was built in Cumbria, Britain. Temples have since been built in Canada, the USA, Spain and Brazil.

Western Buddhists take part in a Tibetan Buddhist ceremony in Dharamsala.

FRIENDS OF THE WESTERN BUDDHIST ORDER

The Friends of the Western Buddhist Order (FWBO) was started in 1967 by an English Buddhist monk, Venerable Sangharakshita (born Denis Lingwood). During World War II, he was stationed in India and Sri Lanka. He stayed on in Asia after the war and was ordained a Theravada monk. He also studied Tibetan and Chan Buddhism. He decided to form a Buddhist movement that combined elements of these traditions in a way that suited Western society. For example, the FWBO does not have monks and nuns. Highly committed Buddhists take vows and are ordained as 'members'. They do not wear robes but have a scarf, called a *kesa*, for special ceremonies.

The future of Buddhism

Buddhism faces a number of challenges as it looks to the future. In its Asian heartland, the 20th century proved a time of mixed fortunes. In some countries, Buddhists faced persecution under brutal governments. In others, war and national unrest put Buddhism under threat. Recently, however, Buddhism has begun to re-establish itself in countries such as India and Indonesia. It is also gaining new followers in non-Asian countries, especially in Europe, North America and Australia.

In some traditionally Buddhist countries, such as Thailand and Sri Lanka, the values and teachings of Buddhism – including non-attachment to material possessions – are being undermined by the emergence of Western-style consumerism. In the West, where Buddhism has arrived more recently, it is precisely these values that have attracted new followers.

But what lies in store for Buddhism? A key Buddhist teaching states that nothing stays the same for ever; everything is always changing. If Buddhism can continue to adapt to different cultures and circumstances, its future is likely to be healthy and bright.

Buddhist monks protest against an alcohol company in Bangkok, Thailand.

CHAPTER 6
SIKHISM

THE SIKH religion began in India at the end of the 15th century. It was founded by a teacher called Guru Nanak. Nanak lived in Punjab, a fertile region of north-west India between the Himalaya Mountains and the River Ganges. In the 15th century, the Punjab region was an important centre of Hinduism, but it was controlled by Muslim rulers. This meant that Nanak grew up in close contact with two great religions. From an early age, he studied Hinduism and Islam. He also spent time on his own, thinking about the nature of God. Later, he founded a new religion based on everything he had learnt. Because of his wisdom, Nanak was given the title 'guru', or 'teacher' in Sanskrit.

Nanak's early life Nanak was born in 1469 in the Punjabi village of Talwandi, about 80 kilometres south-west of the city of Lahore in what is now Pakistan. His birthplace was later renamed Nankana Sahib, meaning 'the Lord Nanak', in honour of the founder of the Sikh faith. Nanak's family were Hindus, but his father managed the accounts of a local Muslim landlord.

There are many stories about the early life of Guru Nanak, all of them illustrating the fact that he was a remarkable child. One story tells how the he was born with a powerful sense of holiness, which was immediately recognized both by the Muslim midwife and the Hindu priest who were present at his birth. The priest prepared a horoscope for the boy, which predicted that Hindus and Muslims alike would come to recognize Nanak as a great thinker and teacher.

Once he reached school age, Nanak astonished all his teachers with his wisdom and understanding. At the age of seven he started composing hymns, which expressed his own beliefs. Like all his fellow students, Nanak spoke Punjabi, which was a purely spoken language without any written form. However, by the time he was a teenager he had also mastered three written languages: Sanskrit, the ancient language of the Hindu texts; and Arabic and Persian, the languages of Islam.

In the 15th century, Hindu society was ruled by the rigid caste system. This ancient, hereditary system divided people into four main castes, or classes. Nanak's family belonged to the *kshatriya*, or warrior caste, but he rejected this way of dividing and judging people. When he was 11 years old, Nanak refused to take part in the ceremony to welcome him to his caste. Instead of accepting the *janeu*, a sacred thread that showed he was a Kshatriya, he challenged the priest who offered it to him. In front of his whole family Nanak asked the question: shouldn't people earn respect through their actions, rather than by wearing a sacred thread? This was the start of a lifetime's teaching on the equality of all people.

Studying Hinduism

Nanak was educated as a Hindu and learnt all the teachings of his faith. He attended school where he was taught by priests, and he also talked to wandering Hindu holy men. One branch of Hinduism had a special appeal for Nanak. This was the *bhakti*

The birthplace of Guru Nanak in Talwandi has been turned into a Sikh shrine. Many Sikhs make a pilgrimage to worship there.

movement, which had developed in the 13th century. Its followers ignore caste and concentrate on devotion to a personal god. Nanak later adopted the idea of a personal god in his hymns. However, the Sikhs' god does not take a human form, like the god of the bhaktis.

India in around 1460, showing the main Hindu kingdoms and the Muslim Lodhi lands.

EVERYONE IS EQUAL

Sikhs believe that all human beings are equal – male and female, young and old, rich and poor. This is because they believe that all people are equally loved by God.

Though they say there are four castes,
One God created all men
All men are moulded of the same clay.
The Great Potter has merely varied their
*   shapes.*

Hymn from the Sikhs' holy book,
the Guru Granth Sahib.

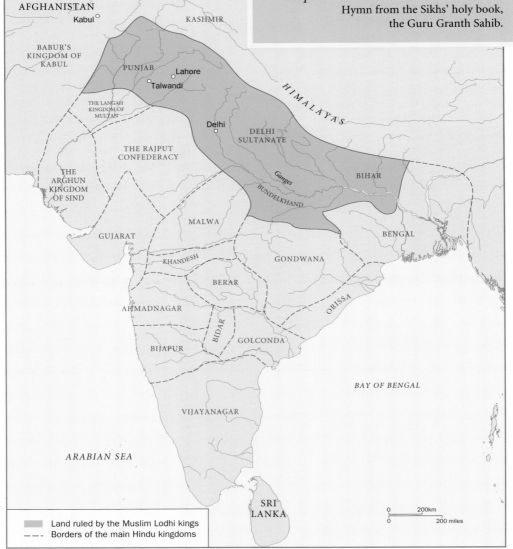

Land ruled by the Muslim Lodhi kings
- - - Borders of the main Hindu kingdoms

Studying Islam As Nanak grew up, he observed Muslims practising their religion. He discussed Islamic beliefs with Muslim scholars and studied their holy book, the Qur'an. Nanak was especially interested in Sufism, a branch of Islam that had begun in Persia. Sufis lead a simple life and meditate on the nature of God. Nanak admired the mystical nature of the Sufis. He aimed to achieve a similar state of understanding through his own religious practices.

Sultanpur When he was about 16 years old, Nanak left the village of Talwandi and set off for Sultanpur, a small town close to the Sutlej River. Nanak's married sister lived there and she helped her brother get a job as a tax collector for a local Muslim ruler. Over the next eight years, he combined his work with religious studies, and began to attract a group of followers. During this time, Nanak also married a Hindu girl, Sulakhni, and had

ONE GOD

Although he disagreed with many Muslim teachings, Nanak was impressed by the Muslim belief in a single God. He found this belief much more convincing than the Hindus' devotion to many gods. Sikhs believe in a single, supreme God. During their services, they chant the words *Ik Onkar*, which mean, 'There is only one God'.

two sons. Meanwhile, his fame was spreading. A large group of followers arrived in Sultanpur to join with Nanak in his hymns, prayers and contemplation.

Travels After eight years in Sultanpur, Nanak became restless. He decided it was time to meet new people and to learn what they looked for in their faith. So,

The area where Sikhism began was originally Hindu, but in the 11th century it was invaded by Muslims. This minaret (prayer tower) was built in Delhi to celebrate a Muslim victory over the Hindus. Work began on the minaret – the Qutub Minar – in 1193.

in the summer of 1496, he set off on a series of journeys. It is not certain exactly where Nanak went, but most accounts agree that he first headed east towards the ancient cities of Haridwar and Varanasi. Next, he travelled widely in the regions of Assam and Orissa in northern India. These were all holy Hindu places, with magnificent shrines and libraries. Here, Nanak shared ideas with pilgrims, scholars and mystics.

A map of important places in Guru Nanak's early life.

According to the legends, after he left the north, Nanak visited the great Hindu kingdoms of southern India. While in the south, he is said to have also crossed to the island of Sri Lanka where the religion of Buddhism was practised.

As he travelled through India, Nanak spread his ideas, sometimes preaching in a Hindu temple, sometimes in a mosque, and sometimes in the open air. He also called at people's houses and joined them in singing the hymns he had composed.

Later in his life, Guru Nanak travelled beyond India in search of greater understanding. According to legend, he travelled to the Muslim cities of Kabul, Makkah and Baghdad. He may also have visited the Buddhist monasteries of Tibet. Wherever he went, he observed the practices of the different religions. He spoke to ordinary worshippers, studied holy texts, and discussed ideas with scholars.

OFFERINGS TO GOD

One story tells of a meeting in the Hindu city of Haridwar, where a group of Hindu priests explained to Nanak their practice of sacrificing animals for their gods. Nanak listened carefully, then responded: 'The sacrifices ... of this age should consist in giving food to those who repeat God's name and practise humility.'

A Sikh boy reads from the Sikhs' holy book, the Guru Granth Sahib. Like all Sikh texts, it is written in the Gurmukhi script, a language created by Guru Nanak.

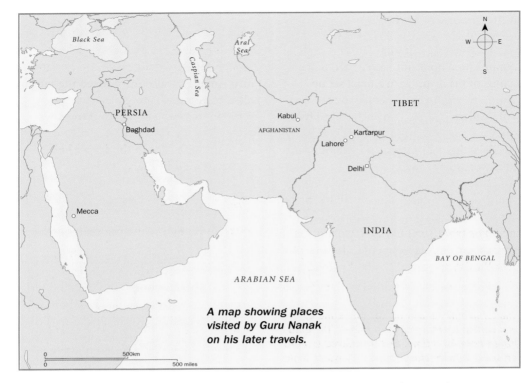

A map showing places visited by Guru Nanak on his later travels.

Hymns

After his travels, Guru Nanak returned to Punjab, where he found a peaceful spot on the Ravi River, north of the city of Lahore, and built the village of Kartarpur. Nanak spent the last 15 years of his life at Kartarpur, trying to form a new religion from the essential elements of everything he had learnt. In these peaceful years, Guru Nanak wrote a collection of hymns that became the basis of the new faith. In his hymns, Guru Nanak taught that there is only one God, and that all human beings are equal. He encouraged his followers to devote their lives to God. He also taught that people should be prepared to work hard in the service of God and their fellow human beings. Nanak's 974 hymns were later collected in the Sikhs' holy book, the Guru Granth Sahib.

The first Sikhs

Many followers flocked to Kartarpur to be close to Guru Nanak. These people became known as 'sikhs', which comes from the Sanskrit word for 'follower'. The Sikhs came from a range of castes and faiths. One of Guru Nanak's closest companions was a Muslim called Mardana. He abandoned his Muslim faith to join Nanak early in his travels, and accompanied the guru for the rest of his life.

At Kartarpur, Nanak started the practice of sharing a meal with anyone who came to hear him preach. After the service, everybody joined in a shared meal, known as the *langar*. This was a way of rejecting the caste system, which did not allow members of different castes to eat together.

Continuing the work

Guru Nanak died in 1539, but before his death he chose a new teacher to continue his work. This was Guru Angad, a very learned man who lived in the small village of Khadur, south of Amritsar, close to the Beas River. Guru Angad spent the next 13 years teaching the Sikh religion. He collected all Guru Nanak's hymns into a book and also added 62 new hymns of his own. Guru Angad set up schools to teach young people to read and write Gurmukhi. He also encouraged his followers to take part in sports. He taught the Sikhs that a healthy mind and body are both pleasing to God.

Guru Angad chose Amar Das, one of his most devoted followers, to be the third guru. Guru Amar Das was leader of the Sikhs from 1552 to 1574. During his time as guru he sent out his followers all over Punjab to spread the faith. He also established a centre for Sikhs at Goindwal,

This temple in Pancha Sahib, near Lahore, was built in memory of Guru Nanak. The guru stayed here for a time, and is believed to have left his handprint close to the holy water tank.

on the banks of the Beas River. Guru Amar Das held celebrations at Goindwal three times a year and encouraged Sikhs throughout Punjab to come and join him. Guru Amar Das also introduced the *langar* hall, a communal eating place where everyone shared a simple meal together. Anyone who came to visit Guru Amar Das had to eat with him in the *langar* hall, the practice started by Guru Nanak.

A NEW LANGUAGE

When Guru Nanak preached to his followers, he used the local language of Punjabi. However, this was just a spoken language. Nanak was faced with the problem of what language to use for his written texts. He did not want to use Sanskrit (the holy language of the Hindus), or Arabic or Persian (the languages of Islam). So he decided to create a new written language based on Punjabi. This language is called Gurmukhi, which means 'from the guru's mouth'. It is still used today for all the Sikhs' holy texts.

The temple at Amritsar Before he died, Guru Amar Das chose a site for a special temple for the Sikhs. He decided that the temple should be built at the village of Amritsar. The site was chosen for its beautiful position on the shores of a lake, surrounded by forests. In 1574, Guru Ram Das became the fourth guru. He was an outstanding Sikh and the husband of the third guru's younger daughter. Guru Ram Das led the Sikhs for the next seven years. During this time, he devoted himself to the job of building the temple at Amritsar. In 1581, Guru Ram Das was succeeded by his son, Guru Arjan, and from this time onwards gurus usually chose their sons to succeed them. Guru Arjan led the Sikhs until 1606 and completed the temple at Amritsar. This stunning building, constructed on an island, later became known as the Golden Temple.

A holy book Guru Arjan also compiled a holy book for the Sikhs. He collected the hymns of the first four gurus and added some new hymns of his own. He also chose some writings by Muslim and Hindu holy men. The book became

Guru Arjan, the fifth guru. After his tragic death, many Sikhs decided that they must fight to defend their religion.

known as the *Adi Granth* ('first book'). In 1604, Guru Arjan installed the original copy of *Adi Granth* in a place of honour in the temple at Amritsar.

Mughal emperors Less than two years after the *Adi Granth* was installed at Amritsar, Guru Arjan was arrested by the Mughal emperor Jahangir. The Mughals were Muslims from Afghanistan, who had seized control of Delhi in 1526. Their leader, Babur, declared himself the first Mughal emperor, and his son Akbar built up a vast empire that covered northern India. Akbar was a wise and tolerant ruler, who was interested

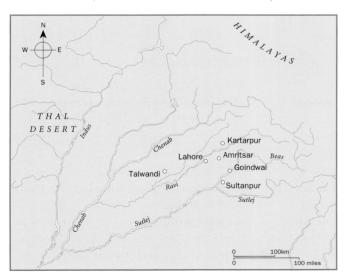

A map of the Sikh heartland in around 1580.

The Harimandir Sahib, or Golden Temple, at Amritsar is part of a complex of religious buildings (see plan on page 198). Completed in 1604, the temple is the holiest part of the complex.

THE DUTY OF SEVA

The gurus did not merely plan the layout of the temple at Amritsar, they also helped with the physical work of digging and construction. Sikhs believe that they should serve God by performing simple physical tasks. The name for this service is *seva*, and by performing it, Sikhs show that they are humble before God. Today, Sikhs perform the duty of seva by helping out in their temple. They take turns to keep the temple clean. They also cook and serve a simple meal for everyone to share in the *langar* hall.

in learning about all religions. However, his son and successor, Jahangir, was a very cruel man, determined to make Islam the only religion of the Mughal Empire.

In 1606, Jahangir's son Ksuru rose in revolt against his father. Jahangir defeated the rebellion and dealt out violent punishments to all his son's supporters. Unluckily for the Sikhs, Ksuru had once met Guru Arjan, so Jahangir decided that the guru was involved in his son's revolt. Jahangir gave orders that the holy man should be arrested and put to death by torture. It was a terrible death. The guru was seated on a hot iron plate while burning sand was poured all over him. Then he was immersed in near-boiling water, and finally he was drowned in the Ravi River. However, the guru did not protest about these agonies. Later, his Sufi friend Mian Mir recorded some of the guru's last words: 'I bear all this torture to set an example to the teachers of the True Name, that they may not lose patience or complain to God in their sufferings.'

Guru Hargobind

Guru Hargobind The torture and death of Guru Arjan marked a dramatic turning point in the history of the Sikhs. His followers responded to the news of their leader's death with rage. This shocking incident changed Sikhism from a peaceful religious faith into a warrior movement. It was the start of 150 years of warfare against the Mughals and other Islamic forces.

Guru Hargobind, eldest son of Guru Arjan, was only 11 when he succeeded his father, but he immediately began the task of building up an army to fight the Mughals. In 1628, the Sikhs and Mughals clashed for the first time. The battle, fought close to Amritsar, lasted for two days and the Mughal army was defeated. Hargobind realized that if he stayed in Amritsar, the temple would be in danger, so he left the holy city and took to the hills. After that, he never saw Amritsar again.

GURDWARAS

Guru Hargobind spent most of his life travelling, but he needed a place in which to meet with other Sikhs, so he established the *gurdwara*, where Sikhs could pray and read from their holy book. Gurdwara means 'the door to the guru'. Today, Sikhs all over the world meet in gurdwaras. These do not need to be grand buildings, but can be any place where the Sikh holy book is kept and where Sikhs meet to worship. Some gurdwaras are simply a special room in a Sikh's private house.

Sikhs arrive to celebrate a festival at the temple in Anandpur Sahib. The temple was built close to Kiratpur, in memory of Guru Hargobind.

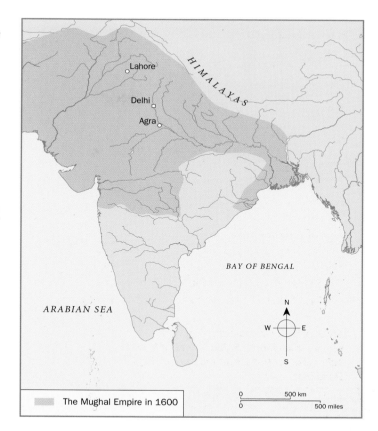

The Mughal Empire in 1600, showing the major centres of Muslim rule.

The Mughal Empire in 1600

Two further battles followed – at Lahira, in southern Punjab, in 1631 and at Kartarpur, near Amritsar, in 1634. Both ended in victory for the Sikhs. These victories angered the Mughals even more, and Guru Hargobind spent the rest of his life fighting off Mughal attacks.

Guru Hargobind lived a nomadic life, visiting Sikhs all over the Punjab region. However, towards the end of his life, he settled in Kiratpur, in the foothills of the Himalayas. It later became the site of Anandpur Sahib, a famous Sikh temple.

Guru Tegh Bahadur

After Guru Hargobind's death in 1644, there was a period of relative calm. This lasted until 1675 when one of Hargobind's successors, the ninth guru, Tegh Bahadur, was forced to take a stand against another Mughal emperor, Aurangzeb. The emperor was determined to wipe out all religions except Islam, and when he gave orders for the Hindu temples of Kashmir to be destroyed, the Hindus appealed to Tegh Bahadur for help. Believing that he would be able to talk to Emperor Aurangzeb reasonably, Tegh Bahadur set off on his own to meet him. But the emperor had other ideas. On his way to Delhi, Tegh Bahadur was arrested by the emperor's troops and brought to the city in an iron cage. The emperor ordered him to convert to Islam. For the next five days Tegh Bahadur was tortured, but he refused to alter his religious beliefs, and eventually he was beheaded. The spot where he died later became the site of Sis Ganj, a Sikh gurdwara.

Guru Gobind Singh
The tenth guru was Tegh Bhadur's son, Gobind Singh. Although only nine years old when his father died, he was determined to defend the Sikh faith against its enemies. He established a strong base for the Sikhs in the mountain city of Anandpur in the foothills of the Himalayas. He also studied many holy texts so that he could become a wise spiritual leader for his people. In 1685, at the age of 19, Guru Gobind Singh took full charge of the Sikhs.

In the early years of his leadership, Gobind Singh fought off several attacks on Anandpur, but in 1704 a powerful Mughal army forced the Sikhs to leave their city. Emperor Aurangzeb promised the Sikhs that they could leave Anandpur in safety, but he broke his word. Some of the emperor's troops attacked the retreating Sikhs, brutally killing men, women and children.

After leaving Anandpur, Gobind Singh stayed in Dina in present-day Pakistan. He then moved to Talwandi Sabo, south of the Sutlej River. Here, in this peaceful place, later renamed Damdama Sahib, he completed the final version of the Sikh's holy book, the Guru Granth Sahib.

While he was in Dina, Gobind Singh also wrote two famous letters to

> ## SINGH AND KAUR
> Guru Gobind Singh said that all Sikh males should take the name 'Singh', and all Sikh females should be named 'Kaur'. Singh means 'lion' and Kaur means 'princess'. Today, many Sikh men and women still take the names Singh and Kaur.

Aurangzeb, publicly blaming him for being untrue to the ideals of the Muslim religion. Surprisingly, these letters impressed Aurangzeb to the extent that he instructed his deputy to make peace with Gobind Singh.

The eleventh guru
In 1707, Emperor Aurangzeb was succeeded by his son, Emperor Bahadur Shah. Guru Gobind Singh went to meet him in Agra, on the banks of the Yamuna River in northern India, and together they travelled south. Gobind Singh hoped that the emperor would allow the Sikhs to return to Anandpur. However, by the time they reached the town of Nanded, on the banks of the Godavari River, it was evident that this would not happen. So Gobind Singh decided to make his base in Nanded instead.

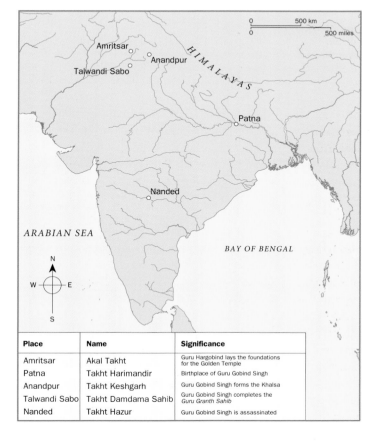

The Five Takhts: The Sikhs built the Five Takhts (special temples) to mark the places where major events in their history took place. Four of them are connected with the life of Guru Gobind Singh.

Place	Name	Significance
Amritsar	Akal Takht	Guru Hargobind lays the foundations for the Golden Temple
Patna	Takht Harimandir	Birthplace of Guru Gobind Singh
Anandpur	Takht Keshgarh	Guru Gobind Singh forms the Khalsa
Talwandi Sabo	Takht Damdama Sahib	Guru Gobind Singh completes the *Guru Granth Sahib*
Nanded	Takht Hazur	Guru Gobind Singh is assassinated

This painting shows the origins of the Khalsa *ceremony. Here, the five founders of the Khalsa gather in front of Guru Gobind Singh. One of them offers the sacred food of* Karah Parshad *(sacred pudding) to the guru.*

Many people flocked to Nanded to hear the teachings of Gobind Singh, and the town became a centre for Sikhism in southern India. However, this peaceful time did not last long. In 1708, jealous of the power of Gobind Singh, the local Muslim governor sent two assassins to murder him. The guru survived the attack but died soon afterwards. As he lay dying, Gobind Singh announced that there should be no more gurus after him. Realizing that the Sikhs would quarrel among themselves about who should be their next leader, he explained that they should treat their holy book as their guru. Whenever they needed advice, they should turn to the Guru Granth Sahib.

Today, the Guru Granth Sahib is often known as the eleventh guru. Copies of

THE KHALSA

In 1699, Guru Gobind Singh held a dramatic ceremony. He asked for volunteers who were prepared to die for their faith to step into his tent. Five men volunteered. They became the first members of a group of devout Sikhs known as the Khalsa. The Khalsa continues to this day. Its members promise to obey the rules of the Sikh religion. They wear five symbols to remind them of their promise:

- *kesh* – uncut hair
- *kara* – a steel bangle on the right wrist
- *kangha* – a wooden comb
- *kachera* – cotton underwear
- *kirpan* – a steel sword

the book are treated with great respect, as if it were a living teacher. It is the focus of worship in the gurdwaras, and usually rests on cushions on a raised platform beneath a canopy.

The 18th century Following the death of Guru Gobind Singh, Banda Singh emerged as the military leader of the Sikhs. He gathered a small army and marched towards the town of Samana in eastern Punjab. Banda's army captured Samana from its Mughal rulers and went on to seize more than a dozen towns. Banda then chose the fortress at Mukhlispur, halfway between Sadhaura and Nahan, as his base. He renamed the fortress Lohgarh and made it the capital of a new Sikh state. This was the first time that Sikhs had claimed land as their own.

In August 1710, the Mughal emperor decided to strike back. A vast Muslim army descended on Punjab and there were bloody battles at Sadhaura, Sirhind and Lohgarh. Over the next five years, Banda and his followers fought a determined campaign, winning cities from the Mughals but then losing them again. Eventually, in 1715, they were defeated. Banda was taken prisoner and hundreds of Sikhs were executed. But Banda had left a legacy in Punjab. Although the Mughals kept control of some key towns, the idea of a Sikh state had been born.

For the rest of the 18th century, the Sikhs had to face persecution by the Mughals and also invasion from Afghanistan. Between the years 1748 and 1764, Afghan armies invaded India eight times, and each time they marched through Punjab, causing death and destruction. Most distressing of all for the Sikhs, the Afghans attacked the temple at Amritsar on three occasions.

The British in India In spite of all their troubles in the 18th century, by the 1800s the Sikhs were in a strong position. The Mughal Empire had been growing steadily weaker, allowing the Sikhs to gain

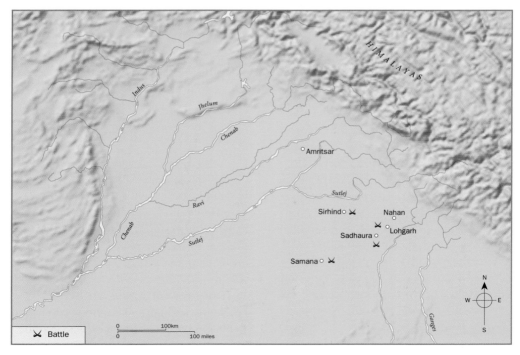

A map showing key places in the military campaigns of Banda Singh.

The Sikh flag, the Nishan Sahib, *plays a central part in all Sikh ceremonies. The* khanda *symbol at the centre of the flag reminds Sikhs to be strong and brave, and to fight for freedom and justice. These ideas have been very important in Sikh history.*

THE SIKH FLAG

Wherever the Sikhs conquered, they flew their flag. This flag, known as the Nishan Sahib, is still flown outside gurdwaras today. At the centre is the *khanda*, a symbol consisting of a circle with a double-edged sword at its centre and two curved swords on either side. The circle reminds Sikhs that there is only one God, who has no beginning and no end. The double-edged sword stands for freedom and justice, while the two curved swords remind Sikhs to be strong, both in their everyday life and in their beliefs.

control of large parts of eastern Punjab. They also controlled most of western Punjab (present-day Pakistan) and the mountainous areas to the north. However, they were about to face a new challenge in the form of the British East India Company.

Traders from Europe had settled in India as early as the 16th century, and some trading companies became very powerful. By 1800, the British East India Company had gained control of large areas of India and was the real power behind the Mughal emperor. The company maintained a large army to deal with any groups that stood in its way.

Ranjit Singh In 1801, a new leader of the Sikhs emerged. Ranjit Singh (the Lion of the Punjab) was a brilliant horseman and warrior. He was also very ambitious. In 1799, aged 19, he led an army into Lahore and seized the city from the Muslims. Two years later, he was crowned maharaja (prince) of Punjab. Ranjit Singh was the first Sikh leader to be crowned a royal ruler. He ruled Punjab efficiently and fairly. Muslims and Hindus in his kingdom were treated well, and he appointed several Muslims to important posts in his government.

Meanwhile, Ranjit Singh set about the task of gaining more land. Some territories were won in battle; others were gained by business agreements. In less than ten years, he built up a rich and powerful state in north-west India.

The Treaty of Amritsar

The officials of the British East India Company recognized that the Sikhs were valuable trading partners. Punjab was India's most productive region, both in terms of agriculture and manufactured goods, and the Sikhs ran it very efficiently. However, the British were worried by the ambitions of Ranjit Singh. Instead of challenging the young maharaja directly, they decided to support the claims of some local rulers with lands south of the Sutlej River, who felt threatened by his expansionism. In 1809, the British persuaded Ranjit Singh to sign the Treaty of Amritsar. As part of the terms, he agreed not to conquer any more lands south of the river. In return, the British offered him their 'perpetual friendship'. Ranjit Singh agreed to the terms because he needed to keep the British as his allies while he tried to gain more land in the north.

Sikhs celebrate Hola Mohalla *in Anandpur, Punjab. Today, this colourful ceremony reminds Sikhs of past battles for their faith.*

HOLA MOHALLA

Sikhs aim to live peaceful lives, but they also believe that they should be prepared to fight for what they think is right. In the 17th century, Guru Gobind Singh introduced a spring festival known as Hola Mohalla. In this festival Sikhs were trained to use weapons so that they could be prepared for war. Today, Sikhs still celebrate Hola Mohalla, but now they hold sporting activities and competitions.

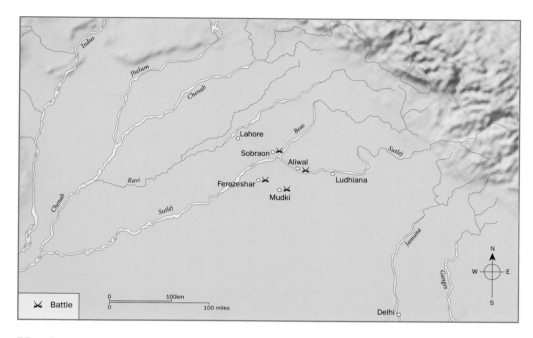

The key sites in the First Anglo-Sikh War (1845–1846).

Moving north

After he had signed the Treaty of Amritsar, Ranjit Singh concentrated his efforts on the areas to the north and west of Punjab. As the Sikh army advanced on these regions, many rulers appealed to the British for help. However, the British were obliged to ignore their pleas because of the terms of the Treaty of Amritsar. Over the next 20 years, Ranjit Singh succeeded in driving the Afghans from many territories in the north-west. By 1839, the Sikhs had expanded their kingdom to include some rich northern regions, including the kingdom of Kashmir and the areas around the cities of Peshawar and Kabul.

The First Anglo-Sikh War

In 1839, Ranjit Singh died suddenly at the age of 58. During his lifetime, he had built up a great Sikh kingdom. However, none of his sons had the qualities of a great leader, and over the next five years the Sikh government in Lahore slid into chaos. In 1844, the British took advantage of the Sikhs' weakness. They arrived with a massive army and camped just south of the Sutlej River, waiting for a chance to attack the Sikhs.

In November 1845, the British seized two Sikh villages near Ludhiana, south of the river, claiming that they were sheltering criminals. When a Sikh army crossed the river to take back the villages, the British immediately declared war, on the grounds that the Sikhs had broken the terms of the Treaty of Amritsar. This was the start of the First Anglo-Sikh War. Over the next four months, the Sikhs fought the British in four battles. They were defeated each time, and thousands of their soldiers were killed. Although the Sikhs fought bravely, they were let down by weak leadership. After the final battle, the British marched straight to Lahore to make an agreement with the Sikh government.

The Treaty of Lahore

The Treaty of Lahore was signed in March 1846. Under its terms, all the territories south of the Sutlej River were handed over to the British. The British also gained the land that lay between the Sutlej and Beas rivers. This fertile region, called Jullundur Doab, covered an area of 29,525 square kilometres.

A large part of the Sikh kingdom went to Gulab Singh, the non-Sikh ruler of the northern kingdom of Jammu, who had made a secret alliance with the British during the war. As a reward for his cooperation, he was given a large stretch of land in the north of Punjab. He also gained the northern kingdom of Kashmir. This had been handed to the British in the Treaty of Lahore, but very soon after signing the treaty, they sold Kashmir to Gulab Singh for the sum of £1 million. The Treaty of Lahore left the Sikhs with less than two-thirds of their original kingdom. They also had to agree to severe reductions in the size of their army, and a payment of £1.5 million to the British.

Sikh resentment

After the First Anglo-Sikh War, British troops stayed on in Lahore. The Sikh government was in chaos, and the British announced that they would look after the Sikh lands until the maharaja, eight-year-old Dalip Singh, came of age. This was greatly resented by the Sikhs. They were further angered by the treatment of Maharani Jind Kaur, the mother of the young Maharaja Dalip Singh. The maharini had a strong personality and many powerful supporters prepared to fight for her and her son.

Sikh and British soldiers engage in fierce hand-to-hand fighting at the Battle of Chillianwala (1849). The battle ended in victory for the Sikhs.

The British viewed her as a threat to their authority and sent her into exile in the city of Varanasi, in British India. Her fortune was greatly reduced and most of her jewellery was confiscated. This humiliating treatment of the mother of their ruler enraged many Sikhs.

In April 1848, a riot broke out at Multan in southern Punjab after the British tried to replace a local ruler with a British governor. British troops marched on Multan, and the Sikhs united to oppose them. This event was the start of the Second Anglo-Sikh War.

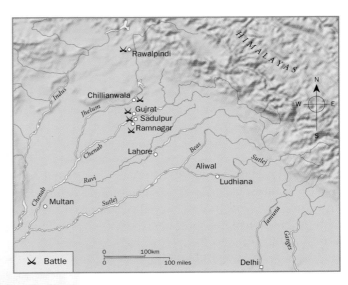

The key sites in the Second Anglo-Sikh War (1848–1849).

The Second Anglo-Sikh War

In the first battle of the war, fought in November 1848 at Ramnagar, near the Chenab River, the Sikhs were greatly outnumbered, yet they managed to defeat the British. Another battle followed at Sadulpur, a few miles further north, but this time there was no obvious winner. However, in January 1849, the Sikhs won a clear victory at Chillianwala, close to the Jhelum River.

BRAVE WARRIORS

The British could not fail to be impressed by the bravery of the Sikh soldiers they were fighting against. The commander of the British troops, Lord Hugh Gough, later described 'the splendid gallantry of our fallen foe' and 'the acts of heroism displayed by the Sikh army'. Gough continued: 'I could have wept to have witnessed the fearful slaughter of so devoted a body of men.'

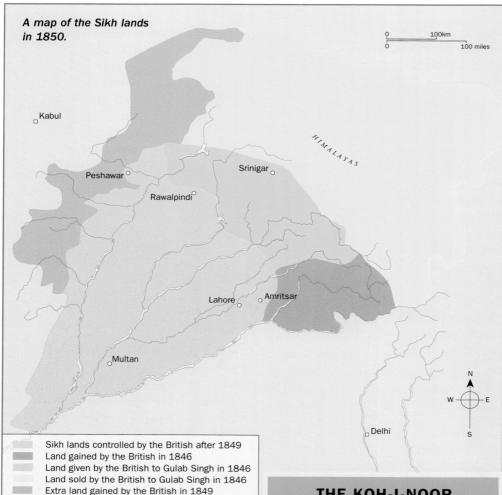

A map of the Sikh lands in 1850.

0 — 100km
0 — 100 miles

Kabul

HIMALAYAS

Peshawar

Srinigar

Rawalpindi

Lahore Amritsar

Multan

N
W — E
S

Delhi

Sikh lands controlled by the British after 1849
Land gained by the British in 1846
Land given by the British to Gulab Singh in 1846
Land sold by the British to Gulab Singh in 1846
Extra land gained by the British in 1849

Shocked and alarmed, the British gathered their forces for the next battle, and in February 1849 a greatly enlarged army faced the Sikhs at Gujrat on the Chenab River, north of Sadulpur. The British had a total force of around 68,000 soldiers while the Sikhs had just 20,000. After two hours of fighting, it was clear that the British were winning, and the Sikhs retreated to the town of Rawalpindi, about 160 kilometres to the north. In March 1849, the Sikhs surrendered Rawalpindi to the British, and the Second Anglo-Sikh War came to an end.

THE KOH-I-NOOR DIAMOND

One of the greatest treasures owned by the young Maharaja Dalip Singh was the famous *Koh-i-noor* diamond, which was said to be the largest diamond in the world. When the British defeated the Sikhs in the Second Anglo-Sikh War, Dalip Singh was forced to surrender the *Koh-i-noor* diamond to Queen Victoria. This famous gem is still owned by the British royal family, but some Sikhs have campaigned to have it returned to India.

The annexation of Punjab

Following the Second Anglo-Sikh War, the British took control of all the Sikhs' lands. By June 1849, Punjab had been divided into 27 districts, each run by a British administrator. The British collected taxes, ran the local police force and the law courts, and kept tight control over all the local farms and industries. In 1858, India became part of the British Empire, and the British tightened their grip on Punjab. They built canals and railways, and the region became a flourishing area for farming and trade. The British also encouraged Sikhs to join the British army, rewarding Sikh soldiers with gifts of land.

Sikh unrest Generally speaking, relations were amicable between the Sikhs and the British, but there were problems, mainly caused by British insensitivity towards the Sikh religion. For example, the British police, who controlled the grounds of the Golden Temple of Amritsar, allowed Hindus to set up their idols there, even though this was against the Sikhs' religious laws.

By the end of World War I (1914–1918), there was also a growing feeling of unrest throughout India. An Indian nationalist movement began a campaign to free India from British rule. One of the leading figures in the movement was the Hindu and former lawyer Mohandas Gandhi. He won many supporters among the Sikhs for his peaceful, non-violent campaign for Indian independence .

The Massacre of Amritsar
The British began to feel that their authority was under threat in Punjab, so when news reached them of a planned nationalist meeting at Amritsar in April 1919, they

Jallianwala Bagh memorial in Amritsar, India.

took action. On 11 April, Brigadier General Reginald Dyer arrived with his troops at Amritsar, and the following day he declared all meetings illegal. On 13 April, the nationalists gathered defiantly at Jallianwala Bagh, an open plot of land close to the Golden Temple. This was also the day when the Sikhs celebrated their spring festival of Baisakhi (see panel on page 194). Many families went to worship at the temple, then moved on to listen to the speeches at Jallianwala Bagh. It was a peaceful gathering, yet Dyer ordered his troops to fire into the crowd. At least 379 men, women and children were killed. The world were horrified by the massacre, but Dyer was unapologetic. He said later that his aim had been to 'strike terror … throughout the Punjab'.

Sikhs take part in the annual spring festival of Baisakhi. The festival involves renewing the Sikh flag and washing the flagpole in yoghurt to cleanse it for the coming year.

Planning for Partition By the 1920s, the situation in Punjab was very tense. The Sikhs had not forgotten the massacre at Amritsar and many of them felt angry about British rule. Meanwhile, throughout India, Indians were campaigning for independence. During the 1930s, as the nationalist movement grew steadily, Muslims and Hindus struggled to agree on how an independent India would be governed. In 1940, the Muslims started to demand the partition of India and the creation of a separate Muslim country. This new country, to be known as Pakistan, would include parts of Afghanistan and the western part of Punjab. It would be

THE FESTIVAL OF BAISAKHI

On the day of the massacre at Amritsar, the Sikhs were celebrating Baisakhi. This festival to welcome the spring was originally adopted from the Hindu religion. It also marks the Sikh New Year and the anniversary of the formation of the Khalsa by Guru Gobind Singh. Baisakhi is still celebrated by Sikhs today. At Baisakhi, the Nishan Sahib flag that flies outside each gurdwara is replaced by a new, clean flag. At the same time, the flagpole is washed in yoghurt, a symbol of purity and cleanliness.

created by dividing the Sikhs' homeland right down the middle.

The Sikhs were bitterly opposed to Partition. To them, the division of Punjab meant the end of their dream of a united and independent Sikh state. In 1946, a group of Sikh leaders presented their grievances to the Muslim leader, Mohammad Ali Jinna. At this meeting, Jinna offered a plan to protect the Sikhs in the new Pakistan, but the Sikhs rejected it. The following day, the Sikhs announced to the press that they would never accept Pakistan. This led to a series of riots in Punjab as Muslims turned on Sikhs. Meanwhile, plans for Partition went ahead. The Sikhs were much smaller in number than the Hindus and Muslims, so their views could be more easily ignored.

The partition of Punjab

On 14 August 1947, the Partition of India took place and the new country of Pakistan came into existence, consisting of West Pakistan and East Pakistan. In the weeks and months that followed, there were terrible massacres in West Pakistan as Muslims tried to drive Sikhs

One of the many meetings held in 1947 to discuss Partition. On the far left is the Sikh representative, Sardar Baldev Singh. Leaning forward over the table is the future prime minister of India, Pandit Nehru.

and Hindus out of their new country. Thousands of Sikhs were ejected from their homes, and many of their shrines and holy places were destroyed. Hundreds of thousands of Sikhs were killed, and nearly 40 per cent of the Sikh community in India became refugees and had to rebuild their lives from nothing. Today, very few Sikhs live in Pakistan, and most of the Sikh holy places in the country are falling into ruins.

Protests It would take many years for the Sikh community to recover from the chaos and destruction of Partition. The Sikhs in East Punjab (ruled by India) were determined to rebuild their lives, and by the end of the 1950s, farming was booming again. By the 1960s, East Punjab was India's main area of rice and wheat production. Meanwhile, the Indian government was offering financial support to new industries in many parts of India, but not East Punjab. Sikhs complained that the government was treating Punjab as 'the breadbasket of India', but not giving it the chance to modernize.

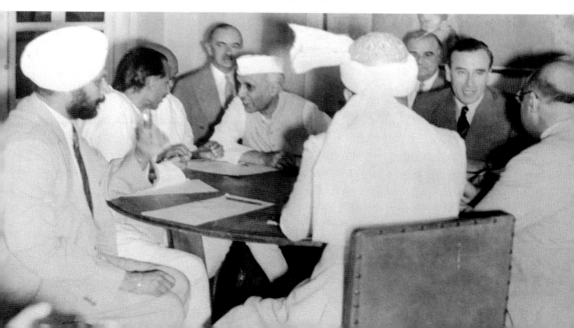

In 1966, the Indian government reorganized East Punjab into three separate districts named Himachal Pradesh, Haryana and Punjab. Most of the Sikhs' holy shrines were in the new Punjab district, so this became their homeland, while the other districts had Hindu rulers. Once again, the Sikhs' lands had been greatly reduced in size.

During the 1970s, anger grew within the

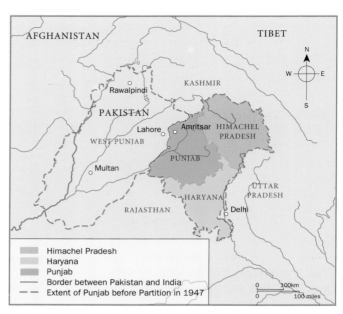

A map showing the Punjab region after 1966.

KHALISTAN

The idea of Khalistan – a separate country for the Sikhs – was born in 1947, when Indian Muslims gained their own country, Pakistan. In the 1980s and 1990s, some Sikh groups used violence in their fight for Khalistan. Today, some Sikhs still campaign for Khalistan, but mainly through peaceful means. The Council of Khalistan is based in Washington, DC, in the USA. This organization tries to gain international support for the creation of an independent Sikh nation.

Sikh community about the government's lack of support for industry, the carving up of the Punjab region, and the lack of Sikh representation in government. Some Sikhs began to voice this anger in protest

Below: *Jarnail Singh Bhindranwhale with a group of followers at the Golden Temple in Amritsar. Bhindranwhale believed that Sikhs should fight to the death for the chance to build their own nation.*

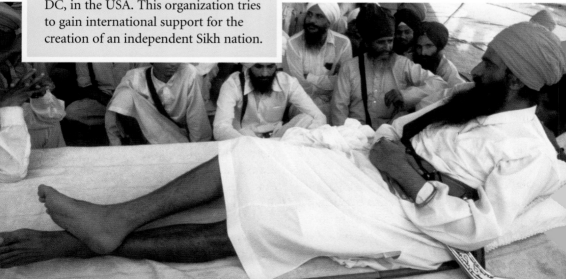

Angry Sikhs take to the streets of Amritsar in June 1984 to protest against sending troops into the Golden Temple.

meetings. They demanded an independent state for the Sikhs, which they named Khalistan, from the word 'Khalsa', the community of Sikhs established by Guru Gobind Singh.

Jarnail Singh Bhindranwhale

One of the leading figures in the campaign for Khalistan was Jarnail Singh Bhindranwhale, a devout but fiery figure, who believed that the Sikhs should be prepared to fight to the death for Khalistan. He was violently opposed to the Indian government, led by Prime Minister Indira Gandhi, a skilful politician, who allowed Bhindranwhale the freedom to speak his mind. He appeared frequently on radio and TV and in the newspapers, and Indians came to believe that he represented all the Sikhs. Many Indians feared that Bhindranwhale was preparing the Sikhs for a violent uprising.

In 1983, Bhindranwhale was accused of organizing a violent protest against the government. He was arrested briefly, then released. After this, he withdrew to the safety of the Golden Temple at Amritsar. Bhindranwhale and a group of followers locked themselves inside a building within the temple complex. They strengthened the building's defences and armed themselves with a small stock of weapons. The stage was set for one of the most terrible events in Sikh history.

Operation Bluestar

In Spring 1984, a group of Sikh protestors publicly burnt a page from the Indian constitution as a symbolic act of defiance against the Indian government. Mrs Gandhi decided it was time to put an end to Sikh resistance. In June 1984, Operation Bluestar went into action: Indian army tanks rolled into the temple complex at Amritsar, and Bhindranwhale and his followers were shot and killed. Many of the temple buildings were damaged and the Akal Takht (one of the Five Takhts, see page 198) was completely destroyed. The army also attacked 37 additional shrines across Punjab, killing hundreds of Sikhs.

Operation Bluestar shocked and angered Sikhs throughout the world. They were especially furious that their holiest shrine had been attacked. On 31 October 1984, two Sikh bodyguards of the prime minister decided to take their revenge. They assassinated Mrs Gandhi in the garden of her home.

Anti-Sikh riots The assassination of Mrs Gandhi sparked a tide of vengeful violence against the Sikhs. All over northern India, Sikhs were attacked, many of them stabbed or burnt alive. In Delhi, the riots lasted for four days and nights, and the government did nothing to stop them. Some Sikhs reacted by forming militant groups, and there were further clashes between Sikhs and Hindus during the 1980s and 1990s.

Sikhs around the world Among the earliest Sikh emigrants were soldiers in the British army. In the 1870s, they began to be sent overseas, stationed in British colonies such as Malaya, Hong Kong and Singapore. Later, they returned to these countries to join the police force or work as security guards. At around the same time, many young Sikh men began to lose patience with land shortages and the lack of jobs in Punjab, and decided their best hope was to leave India. In the 1880s, many Sikhs went to Australia. Some travelled from there to New Zealand and Fiji. Some moved abroad for a few years,

sending money home to their families, before returning to India. Others settled permanently in their new homes. However, Sikh emigration to Australia came to an end in the 1900s when the country placed tougher immigration restrictions.

THE HARIMANDIR SAHIB AND THE AKAL TAKHT

The two most important buildings in the temple complex at Amritsar are the Harimandir Sahib and the Akal Takht. The Harimandir Sahib, or holy shrine, was begun in the 16th century by Guru Arjan. It is the holiest place in the Sikh religion and the home of the original Guru Granth Sahib, the holy book of the Sikhs. Guru Arjan chose to build the Harimandir in the centre of a lake, because the lake – or 'pool of nectar' – symbolizes the spiritual world. The Akal Takht ('the Lord's almighty throne') was built by Guru Hargobind in the 17th century. It is a kind of parliament building where the leaders of the Sikh faith meet to decide on important matters.

Canada and the USA

In 1897, as part of Queen Victoria's Diamond Jubliee celebrations, several British regiments travelled through Canada. This first-hand experience of the country prompted some Sikh members of these regiments to decide to emigrate there. By the early 1900s, many Sikhs

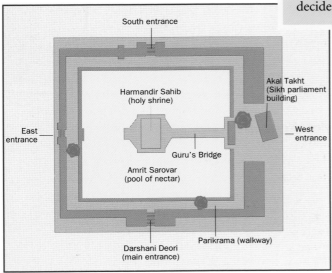

Plan of the temple complex at Amritsar.

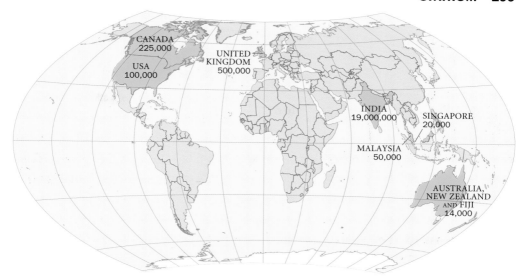

The approximate numbers of Sikhs in some regions of the world today.

were settling in Canada, mainly working as lumberjacks. Around this time, some Sikhs also emigrated to the USA. The first Sikh gurdwara in the USA was built in 1915 in Stockton, California, beside the tracks of the Southern Pacific Railway. The Sikhs became well known for their charity, offering food and shelter to the homeless people walking along the tracks. Large Sikh settlements developed along the west coast of North America, especially in British Columbia, Washington, Oregon and California. In the 1920s, the Canadian and US governments decided to place tough restrictions on Sikh immigration.

East Africa Sikhs played an important role in the industrial development of East Africa. Between 1896 and 1901, Sikh carpenters, blacksmiths and bricklayers travelled there to help build the East African railways. After the

railways were completed, many Sikhs stayed on and other Sikhs joined them there, working as farmers, civil servants and policemen. In 1972, President Idi Amin of Uganda expelled all the Sikhs from his country. Some Ugandan Sikhs returned to India, but many chose to move to Britain.

The Akal Takht, located at the Golden Temple complex, Amritsar. The modern building is a five-storey structure, with marble inlay and a gold-leafed dome.

*Sikh women prepare food in the kitchen of
a UK gurdwara. The UK was one of the first
countries outside India to have a substantial
population of Sikhs.*

Sikhs in the United Kingdom

The first Sikh emigrant to Britain was
Maharaja Dalip Singh, the young Sikh ruler
who lost his throne after the British won
the Second Anglo-Sikh War. He visited
Queen Victoria in 1854 and bought a grand
house in Suffolk. Sikhs began to settle in
the United Kingdom in 1911, and the first
gurdwara in Britain was built that year
in Putney in south-west London. More
Sikhs arrived after World War I, but Sikh
emigration to Britain only really took off in
the 1950s. Most Sikhs settled in Yorkshire,
Lancashire, the Midlands and London.

Jats and non-Jats Two distinct
groups of Sikhs have emerged in the
UK. The early immigrants were mainly
unskilled workers, who had originally
belonged to the Hindu untouchable caste.
In the UK, they often worked as travelling
salesmen, going from house to house with
a suitcase of goods to sell. In the 1950s, a
different group of Sikhs arrived in Britain.
These were mostly from the Jat peasant
caste, people from farming families who
had land of their own in India. The Jats

WESTERN SIKHS

In 1968, a Sikh spiritual teacher, Harbhajan Singh Puri, emigrated from India to Canada to teach yoga. He soon moved to California, where he taught yoga to American students and also explained to them the principles of Sikhism. Before long, he attracted a large group of people who wanted to follow his way of life. They became vegetarians and gave up alcohol, tobacco, drugs and extra-marital sex. They spent part of every day meditating on the Sikh texts. By the end of 1969, some of Harbhajan's students had entered the Sikh religion. They were the first of a growing number of Western Sikhs. Their movement is often known as 3HO, which stands for Healthy, Happy, Holy Organization. They wear white Punjabi clothing and turbans. Today, there are over 10,000 Western Sikhs, based mainly in the USA.

and non-Jats in Britain have often chosen to worship in separate gurdwaras. This division can also be found in Sikh communities in other parts of the world. Many Sikhs are unhappy about the division because it goes against the teachings of Guru Nanak, who rejected the caste system, preaching that all people are equal.

A thriving religion

Even though it was founded only 500 years ago, Sikhism is a major world religion. It is the world's fifth largest faith, after Christianity, Islam, Hinduism and Buddhism. Today there are around 27 million Sikhs worldwide.

A young American Sikh in northern New Mexico. The Western Sikh movement (3HO – Healthy, Happy, Holy Organization) is especially strong in the south-west USA.

TIMELINE

BCE

c. 3000 According to Hindu tradition, Krishna appears on Earth and speaks the *Bhagavad Gita* (Song of God). The Kali yuga (age of iron) begins.

c. 1800 Abraham and his clan leave Ur in Mesopotamia and move to Canaan.

c. 1500–500 The Vedas are composed in the ancient language of Sanskrit.

c. 1000 The kingdom of Israel is established; Saul is the first king.

928 King Solomon dies. The northern Israelite tribes set up the kingdom of Israel; the southern tribes establish Judah.

722 The Assyrians capture Samaria and deport the Israelites.

586 The Babylonians conquer Jerusalem and destroy the Temple; they defeat the kingdom of Judea.

c. 563 Siddhartha Gautama is born in Lumbini, Nepal.

538 King Cyrus the Great of Persia conquers Babylon and allows the Jews living there to return to their homeland.

c. 500 Among Hindus, temple *puja* (worship of the *murti*) becomes popular from this time, and Vishnu, Shiva and Shakti emerge as the main deities.

c. 483 The Buddha passes away in Kushinagara, India.

c. 482 The First Buddhist Council is held at Rajagrha.

c. 373 The Second Buddhist Council is held at Vesali.

c. 321–184 During the Mauryan Empire, the great Hindu epics are written down.

265–232 Buddhism is promoted in India during the reign of Emperor Ashoka.

c. 250 Buddhism is introduced into Sri Lanka.

250 The Third Buddhist Council is held at Pataliputra

164 Judah the Maccabee leads a Jewish rebellion and recaptures Jerusalem.

1st century The Buddhist scripture, the Tipitaka, is written down.

CE

1st century The first images of the Buddha are made in Gandhara; Buddhism reaches China and becomes established in Indonesia.

c. 4 Jesus is born.

c. 28–30 Jesus is a teacher and healer in Palestine, and Christianity begins.

c. 33 Jesus is crucified.

c. 35 St Paul is converted to Christianity.

c. 46 St Paul sets off on the first of his three missionary journeys.

64 Emperor Nero starts to persecute Christians.

c. 65 St Mark completes the first of the Gospels of the New Testament.

70 The Romans conquer Jerusalem and destroy the Second Temple.

100 The Fourth Buddhist Council is held in Kashmir.

132 Simon Bar Kochba leads a Jewish revolt and drives the Romans out of Jerusalem.

135 The Jews are defeated; most are dispersed to different lands.

300s Buddhism probably reaches Korea.

303 Emperor Diocletian begins to persecute Christians.

305 The missionary Frumentius starts to convert the people of Ethiopia to Christianity.

313 The Roman emperor Constantine issues the Edict of Milan, allowing Christians in the empire to follow their religion.

320–550 The Gupta Empire is a golden age for Hindu arts. *The Puranas* are written down.

325 Constantine holds the Council of Nicaea.

c. 350 St Basil establishes a set of rules for monks in the Eastern Church.

391 Emperor Theodosius makes Christianity the official religion of the Roman Empire.

393 The New Testament is completed.

400s The Buddhist university of Nalanda is at its height; Buddhism becomes established in Myanmar.

410	St Augustine of Hippo begins to write *The City of God*.
c. 440	St Patrick starts to convert Irish tribes to Christianity.
c. 500	St Benedict establishes the Benedictine order of monks.
500s	Buddhism becomes established in Vietnam, and reaches Japan from Korea.
500–1000	The Hindu poet-saints of South India compose devotional poems.
597	St Augustine starts to convert the Angles of southern England to Christianity.
600s	Buddhism is introduced into Tibet.
610	Muhammad begins to receive revelations of the Qur'an in Makkah.
622	Muhammad and his followers make the Hijrah to Yathrib (Madinah).
630	Muhammad takes over Makkah.
632	Muhammad dies.
632–661	The first four Islamic caliphs rule.
661–750	The Umayyad dynasty rules the Islamic world.
750–1258	The Abbasid dynasty rules the Islamic world; from 940, the Abbasid caliphs have only symbolic authority.
756	Abd ar-Rahman establishes the Caliphate of Córdoba in Spain.
c. 780–812	The Hindu *acharya* Shankara reestablishes the importance of Hindu texts.
c. 800	The Buddhist monument of Borobodur is built on Java.
909	The first Cluniac monastery is founded.
909–1171	The Shia Fatimids rule in North Africa.
c. 925–1025	The Hindu *acharya* Abhinavagupta lays the foundation for Kashmiri Shaivism.
988	Russia becomes a Christian country.
990–1118	The Islamic Saljuk Empire flourishes.
1017–1137	The Hindu *acharya* Ramanuja advocates that God is ultimately personal.
1054	The Orthodox and Roman Catholic churches split.

1095	Pope Urban II calls Christians to go on the First Crusade.
1098	St Bernard founds the Cistercian order.
1099	The crusaders conquer Jerusalem and establish crusader states in Palestine, Anatolia and Syria.
1100s	Buddhism becomes the religion of Cambodia, and almost disppears from India.
1187	The Muslim leader Salah ad-Din recaptures Jerusalem and founds the Ayyubid dynasty.
1200–1500	Muslims rule northern India. Hindu kingdoms, especially of the Chola dynasty, flourish in southern India.
1206	The Delhi Sultanate is established.
1209	St Francis establishes the first order of Franciscan friars.
1215	St Dominic establishes the Dominican order of monks.
1250	The Mamluk dynasty defeats the Ayyubids and rules Egypt and Syria until 1517.
1256–1335	The Mongols rule Iran and modern-day Iraq.
1258	The Mongols defeat the Abbasids and sack Baghdad.
1290	The Jews are expelled from England.
1309	Pope Clement V moves from Rome to Avignon.
1350	Buddhism becomes the religion of Thailand.
1369–1405	Timur Lane reverses the decline in the Mongol Empire, but it falls apart after his death.
1391–1475	Gedun Truppa is the first Dalai Lama in Tibet.
1394	The Jews are expelled from France.
1453	The Ottoman sultan Mehmet II conquers Constantinople and ends the Byzantine Empire.
1469	Guru Nanak, the founder of Sikhism, is born in Punjab.
1492	The Jews are driven out of Spain.
1502	Shah Ismail founds the Safavid dynasty, which lasts until 1736.
1517	Martin Luther posts his Ninety-five Theses on the church door in Wittenberg.

1520	Martin Luther is excommunicated, marking the start of Lutheranism. Around this time, Guru Nanak sets up the first Sikh community in Kartarpur.
1524	The first major Muslim state in South-East Asia is established in Aceh.
1526	Babur conquers Delhi and founds the Mughal Empire.
1534	King Henry VIII announces that he is supreme head of the Church of England, marking the start of Anglicanism. St Ignatius Loyola founds the Jesuits.
1539	Guru Angad becomes the second guru.
1541	John Calvin establishes the Calvinist Church.
1545–1563	Leaders of the Roman Catholic Church meet at the Council of Trent.
1552	Guru Amar Das becomes the third guru.
1556–1605	Akbar extends Mughal power over most of the Indian subcontinent.
1560s	John Knox founds the Presbyterian Church in Scotland.
1574	Guru Ram Das becomes the fourth guru.
1581	Guru Arjan becomes the fifth guru.
1604	The Sikh temple at Amritsar is completed.
1606	Guru Arjan is tortured and put to death by the Mughal emperor Jahangir. Guru Hargobind becomes the sixth guru.
1612	The Separatists, later known as the Baptists, become established in England.
1618	The Thirty Years' War, between Catholics and Protestants, begins in Germany.
1620	The Pilgrims, a group of Puritans and Separatists, establish a colony in North America.
1631	The Sikhs defeat the Mughals at the Battle of Lahira.
1634	The Sikhs defeat the Mughals at the Battle of Kartarpur.
1644	Guru Har Rai becomes the seventh guru.

1650s	The Society of Friends, later known as the Quakers, is formed.
1661	Guru Har Krishan becomes the eighth guru.
1664	Guru Tegh Bahadur becomes the ninth guru.
1675	Guru Tegh Bahadur is tortured and put to death by the Mughal emperor Aurangzeb. Guru Gobind Singh becomes the tenth guru.
1699	Guru Gobind Singh forms the Khalsa.
c.1706	Guru Gobind Singh completes the *Guru Granth Sahib*.
1708	Guru Gobind Singh dies from an attack by Muslim assassins. Banda Singh starts to win land from the Mughals.
1715	Banda Singh is defeated by the Mughals.
1738	John Wesley begins to preach a new form of Christianity. This marks the start of Methodism.
1739	Nadir Shah invades northern India and sacks Delhi.
1757	After the Battle of Plassey, India comes under British domination.
1779	The Qajar dynasty takes power in Iran.
1801	Ranjit Singh declares himself maharaja of the Punjab.
1808	The sultanate of Sokoto is formed in modern-day northern Nigeria.
1809	Ranjit Singh signs the Treaty of Amritsar with the British.
1828	The Brahmo Samaj is founded, one of many organizations seeking to reform Hinduism, largely in response to European influences.
1830	From this time, many Hindus start migrating to Fiji, Malaysia, Mauritius, the Caribbean, East Africa and South Africa.
1845–1846	The First Anglo-Sikh War ends in victory for the British. The Sikhs and the British sign the Treaty of Lahore.
1848–1849	The Second Anglo-Sikh War ends in victory for the British. The British take over all the Sikhs' lands.
1857	The Indian Revolt against the British in India.

1858	India becomes part of the British Empire.
1861	William Booth founds the Salvation Army.
1869	Mahatma Gandhi, the great Hindu campaigner for Indian independence, is born.
1870s	Sikh emigration from India begins.
1881	The Pali Text Society is founded with the aim of collecting and translating Buddhist texts into English.
1897	The World Zionist Organization is founded.
1900s	The Pentecostal (or Charismatic) movement begins in Los Angeles, USA.
1908	The first Buddhist Society is founded in Britain.
1917	The Balfour Declaration expresses British support for a Jewish homeland in Palestine.
1919	Hundreds of Sikhs are killed in the Massacre of Amritsar.
1928	Hasan al-Banna founds the Society of the Muslim Brothers in Egypt.
1930	The first Buddhist Society is founded in the USA.
1938	During *Kristallnacht*, Jewish property is destroyed all over Germany and Austria.
1943	Jews mount a rebellion against the Nazis in the Warsaw Ghetto uprising.
1947	India gains independence and the country is partitioned between mainly Hindu India and mainly Muslim Pakistan.
1948	The State of Israel is established; around three-quarters of a million Palestinians flee.
1948	The World Council of Churches is founded.
1950s–1970s	Many Hindus migrate to North America (from India), to the UK (from East Africa and India) and to other countries, such as Holland and Australia.
1959	The Dalai Lama is forced to flee from Tibet.

1964	The pope and the patriarch meet in a move to heal divisions between the Roman Catholic and Orthodox churches.
1966	The Punjab region is divided into three states.
1967	Israel and its Arab neighbours clash in the Six-Day War. The whole of Jerusalem falls under Israeli control. The Friends of the Western Buddhist Order (FWBO) is founded.
1970s	The Roman Catholic liberation theology movement begins in South America.
1979	A revolution in Iran leads to Islamic rule under Ayatollah Khomeini.
1984	An Israeli rescue operation brings the Ethiopian Jews to Israel. Indira Gandhi launches Operation Bluestar against the Sikhs. Two Sikhs assassinate Mrs Ghandi, sparking anti-Sikh riots.
1987–1993	The Palestinians wage the First Intifada against Israeli rule.
1989	The Dalai Lama wins the Nobel Peace Prize.
1990	Large numbers of Russian Jews emigrate to Israel following the fall of the USSR.
1994	Israel signs a peace treaty with Jordan.
1996	The Islamist group, the Taliban, take power in Afghanistan.
2000	Christians around the world celebrate two thousand years of Christianity.
2000–2005	The Palestinians wage the Second Intifada against Israel.
2001	Islamist terrorists launch attacks on the USA, killing around 3,000.
2003	The USA leads a war against Iraq and occupies the country.
2014	A group calling themselves Islamic State seizes territory in Iraq and Syria and establishes a new 'caliphate'.

INDEX